virgo

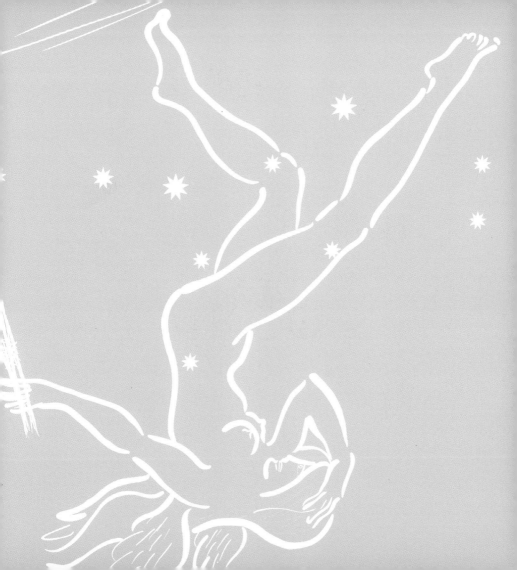

VIRGO

23 August–22 September

PATTY GREENALL & CAT JAVOR

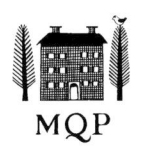

MQP

Published by MQ Publications Limited
12 The Ivories
6–8 Northampton Street
London N1 2HY
Tel: 020 7359 2244
Fax: 020 7359 1616
Email: mail@mqpublications.com
www.mqpublications.com

Illustrations: Gerry Baptist

ISBN: 1-84072-770-5

1 3 5 7 9 0 8 6 4 2

Printed in Italy

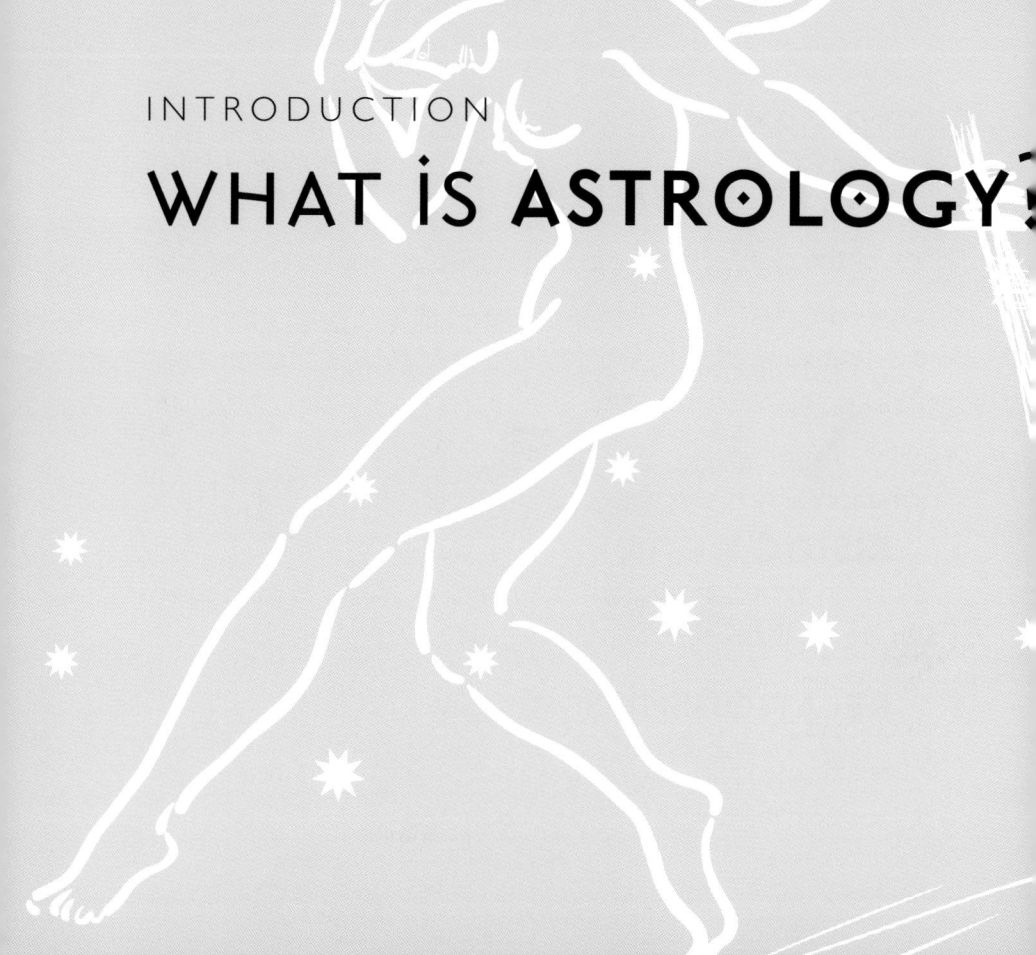

INTRODUCTION

WHAT IS ASTROLOGY?

Astrology is the practice of interpreting the positions and movements of celestial bodies with regard to what they can tell us about life on Earth. In particular it is the study of the cycles of the Sun, Moon, and the planets of our solar system, and their journeys through the twelve signs of the zodiac— Aries, Taurus, Gemini, Cancer, Leo, Virgo, Libra, Scorpio, Sagittarius, Capricorn, Aquarius, and Pisces — all of which provide astrologers with a rich diversity of symbolic information and meaning.

Astrology has been labeled a science, an occult magical practice, a religion, and an art, yet it cannot be confined by any one of these descriptions. Perhaps the best way to describe it is as an evolving tradition.

Throughout the world, for as far back as history can inform us, people have been looking up at the skies and attaching stories and meanings to what they see there. Neolithic peoples in Europe built huge stone

structures such as Stonehenge in southern England in order to plot the cycles of the Sun and Moon, cycles that were so important to a fledgling agricultural society. There are star-lore traditions in the ancient cultures of India, China, South America, and Africa, and among the indigenous people of Australia. The ancient Egyptians plotted the rising of the star Sirius, which marked the annual flooding of the Nile, and in ancient Babylon, astronomer-priests would perform astral divination in the service of their king and country.

Since its early beginnings, astrology has grown, changed, and diversified into a huge body of knowledge that has been added to by many learned men and women throughout history. It has continued to evolve and become richer and more informative, despite periods when it went out of favor because of religious, scientific, and political beliefs.

Offering us a deeper knowledge of ourselves, a profound insight into what motivates, inspires, and, in some cases, hinders, our ability to be truly our authentic selves, astrology equips us better to make the choices and decisions that confront us daily. It is a wonderful tool, which can be applied to daily life and our understanding of the world around us.

The horoscope—or birth chart—is the primary tool of the astrologer and the position of the Sun, Moon, Mercury, Venus, Mars, Jupiter, Saturn,

Uranus, Neptune, and Pluto at the moment a person was born are all considered when one is drawn up. Each planet has its own domain, affinities, and energetic signature, and the aspects or relationships they form to each other when plotted on the horoscope reveal a fascinating array of information. The birth, or Sun, sign is the sign of the zodiac that the Sun was passing through at the time of birth. The energetic signature of the Sun is concerned with a person's sense of uniqueness and self-esteem. To be a vital and creative individual is a fundamental need, and a person's Sun sign represents how that need most happily manifests in that person. This is one of the most important factors taken into account by astrologers. Each of the twelve Sun signs has a myriad of ways in which it can express its core meaning. The more a person learns about their individual Sun sign, the more they can express their own unique identity.

ZODIAC WHEEL

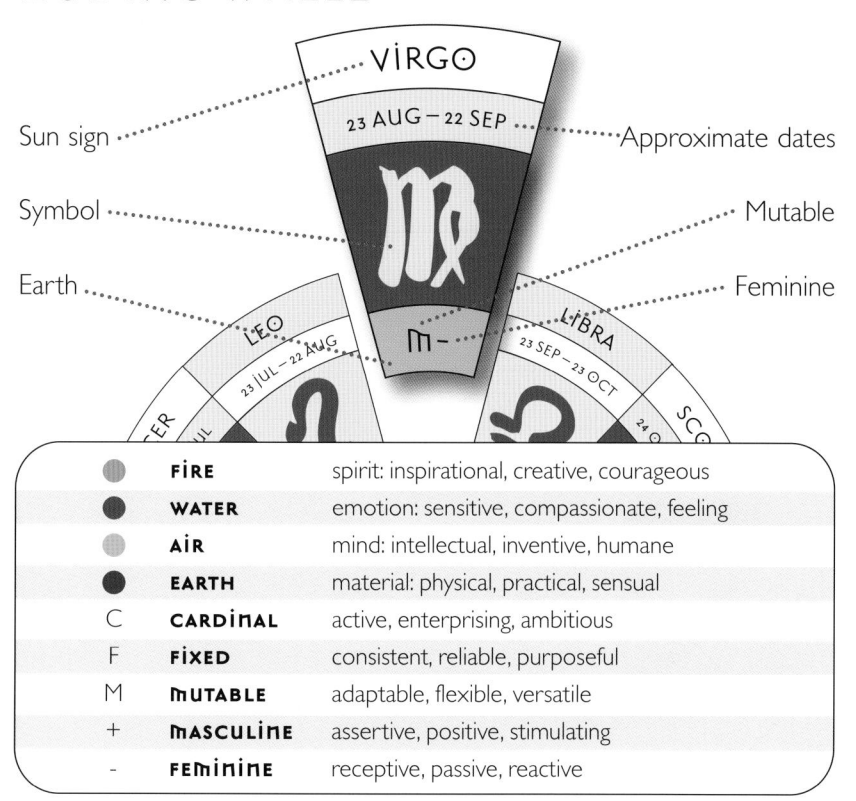

Sun sign ·········· VIRGO

Symbol ··········

Earth ··········

····· Approximate dates

····· Mutable

····· Feminine

●	**FIRE**		spirit: inspirational, creative, courageous
●	**WATER**		emotion: sensitive, compassionate, feeling
●	**AIR**		mind: intellectual, inventive, humane
●	**EARTH**		material: physical, practical, sensual
C	**CARDINAL**		active, enterprising, ambitious
F	**FIXED**		consistent, reliable, purposeful
M	**MUTABLE**		adaptable, flexible, versatile
+	**MASCULINE**		assertive, positive, stimulating
-	**FEMININE**		receptive, passive, reactive

ARİES
21 MAR – 20 APR

TAURUS
21 APR – 21 MAY

PİSCES
20 FEB – 20 MAR

GEMİNİ
22 MAY – 21 JUN

AQUARİUS
21 JAN – 19 FEB

CANCER
22 JUN – 22 JUL

CAPRİCORN
23 DEC – 20 JAN

LEO
23 JUL – 22 AUG

SAGİTTARİUS
23 NOV – 22 DEC

VİRGO
23 AUG – 22 SEP

SCORPİO
24 OCT – 22 NOV

LİBRA
23 SEP – 23 OCT

E–

C+

F–

F+

M+

C–

C–

M+

F+

F–

M+

C+

E–

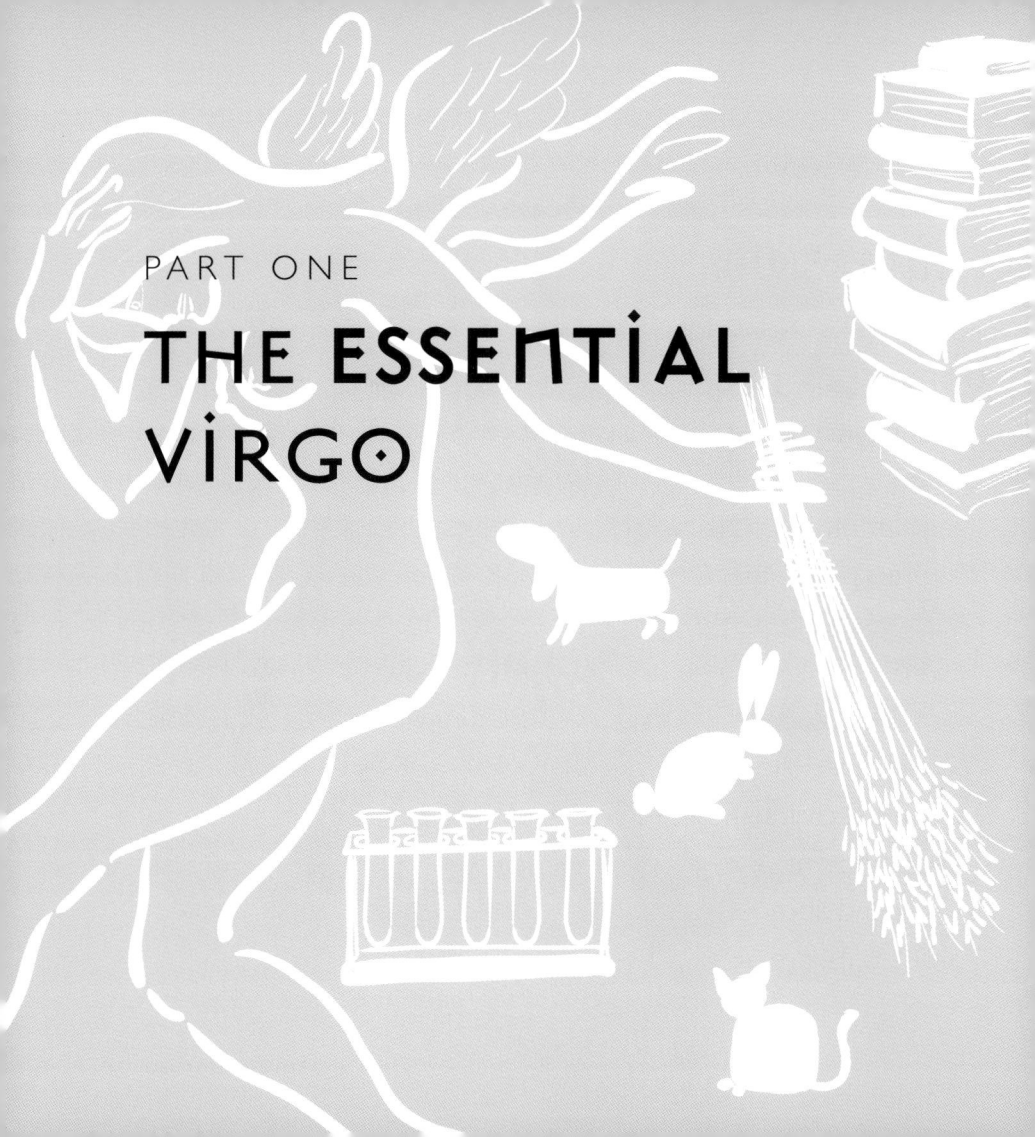

PART ONE

THE ESSENTIAL VIRGO

RULERSHIPS

Virgo is the sixth sign of the zodiac, the second Earth sign, and is ruled by the planet Mercury. Its symbol is the winged Virgin bearing a sheaf of corn. The corn is symbolic of autumn, when Virgo begins, and it signifies harvest time, work, and the attention to detail that is necessary at this time of year. There are earthly correspondences of everything in life for each of the Sun signs. The part of the human body that Virgo represents is the intestines. Virgo is a Mutable and Feminine sign. Gemstones for Virgo are sapphire, carnelian, agate, and tourmaline. Virgo also signifies bookkeepers, accountants, chemists, civil servants, clerks, critics, healers, health workers, and librarians, and the places that Virgo represents are the study and libraries. It is also associated with domestic animals, millet, oats, rye, skullcap, and chicory.

THESE ARE SOME OF THE TRADITIONAL ASSOCIATIONS OF

VIRGO

The part of the human body that Virgo
represents is the intestines.

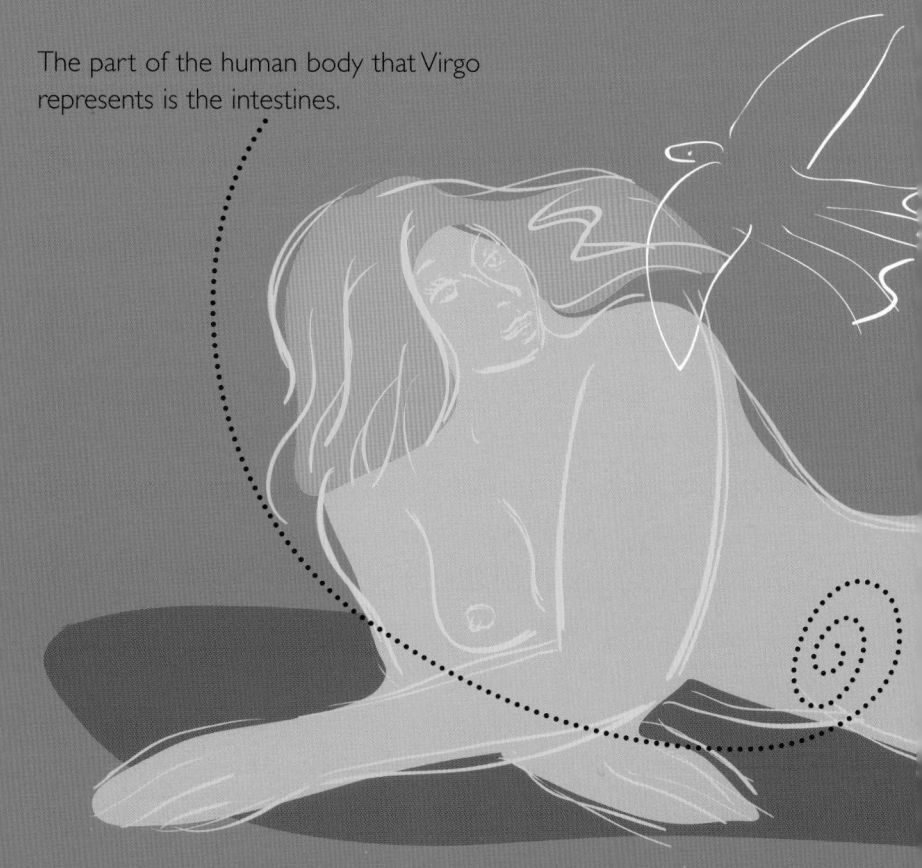

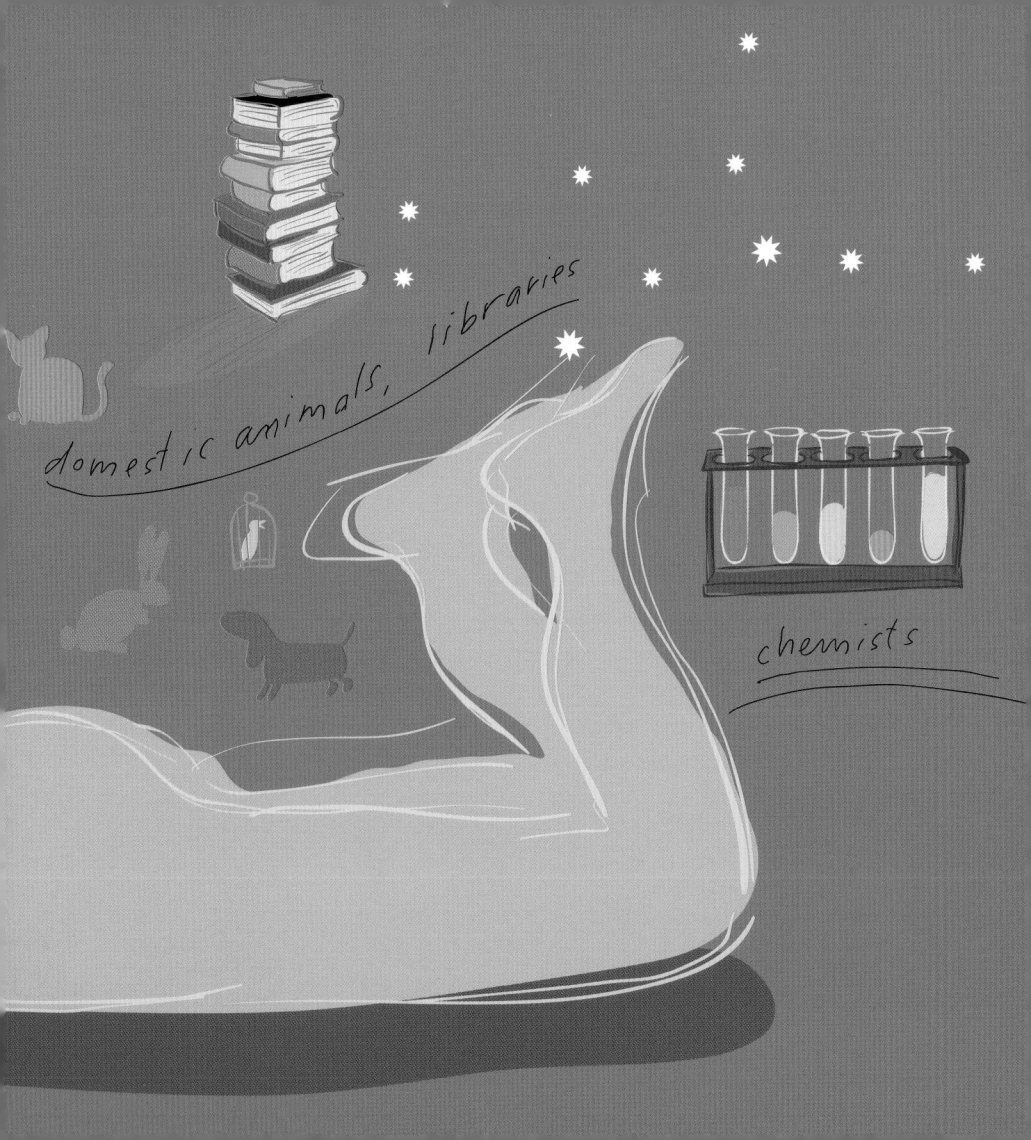

domestic animals, libraries

chemists

PERSOⴖALİTY

Those born under the sign of Virgo are attuned to the perfection of the individual. Through their physical senses and practical abilities they endeavor first to gain an understanding of all the myriad expressions of human talent and then to raise the game to enable the fulfillment of that talent's potential in the material world. This is the reason for Virgo's reputation as the "perfectionist." It's true that they can be finicky, but this stems from their innate ability to grasp the fine and subtle detail that others miss and the way in which they conscientiously apply themselves to weaving everything into a complete, secure whole. Nothing disturbs a Virgo's sense of equilibrium more than having a lot of loose ends that need tying up. Their sense of precision is usually more dominant in one particular area of their life, whether in their work, in the way they complete everyday tasks, or in what they expect from others. They will invest time and energy in ensuring that things operate at optimum efficiency, so that nothing gets in the way or slows down the smooth transition to the next stage.

Basic common sense is another of Virgo's attributes. Confusion is foreign to them; it simply doesn't exist in a Virgo world and when they meet it in others, they find that their logical approach is very much valued. Because of their amazing ability for discernment and for distinguishing what lies at the heart of things, they are great at getting down to the nuts and bolts of a matter. They are also incredibly disciplined, which makes them very successful, but success doesn't go to their heads—their feet are firmly on the

ground, and that keeps them stable. They're people of substance who need to know what lies beneath everything, and they usually do know. If they're not fantastic control freaks already, they have the makings of one! They are also calm yet practical and methodical, and nothing escapes their beady eyes. They are conscientious and will do exactly as is expected of them—and then some—and they won't try to slack off or delegate where they shouldn't.

Virgos' superior analytical skills enable them to see every cog in a wheel as separate, yet still be aware of the entire wheel and its usefulness in assisting progress. And it's the progress toward perfection and the method of getting there that Virgo is all about. They are often modest, serious people, but being ruled by the trickster planet Mercury they also have a rich, earthy sense of humor that can at times be wickedly mischievous. They make wonderful raconteurs, telling fascinating anecdotes that demonstrate their thoughtful, perceptive understanding of life. With their sharp, methodical brain and highly developed physical sensitivity, Virgo is a complex and subtle sign. Its natives can be relied upon to provide a mine of useful information and skills that others seek out to employ for their own ends. Virgo people are usually more than willing to offer their help and expertise, often going above and beyond the call of duty. However, if in some way they aren't realizing their own potential, either in the achievement of a financial return or in the perfection of their personal skills, they will quickly seek another situation in which they can be of assistance. Virgo natives are very adaptable and pragmatic and won't hang around to be used and tossed aside; these people have a finely tuned sense of their own worth and have no desire to see it wasted.

Virgo people also want to hone their skills and talents into the purest and most essential form. Purity and essence are not just intellectual concepts to the discerning Virgo mind. In their attempt to make these reality, they employ their critical facilities and prune away anything that is superfluous. They apply this to their instinctive feel for everything that relates to health and healing, which means that they can be incredibly ruthless when it comes to diet and exercise regimes, believing that, without such ruthlessness, they won't physically be able to complete the tasks they undertake. In fact, many a gym bunny or a health nut is born under the sign of Virgo. They tend to be fit and healthy because they put so much energy into their physical well-being but this is also very much related to their habit of worrying. As well as worrying about being late or about not getting something done, they also construe any little creak or twinge in their body as signifying some terrible complaint. Did someone mention the word "hypochondriac"? When it comes to health matters, Virgos are rather like gardeners tending a garden full of nutritious fruits, vegetables, and herbs. They may, along the way, create a garden of great beauty, but their main purpose is to have a garden that can be healthful for their community.

Virgos have very high expectations of themselves and of others, and although they would never be deliberately hurtful, they will voice their criticism once they have been alerted to someone or something that isn't up to scratch. Virgo people can also be shy; they won't be the pupils who raise their hand in class and shout, "Me, me, me!" Nevertheless, with their bright intellect, they are often the ones who get chosen anyway. Being ruled

by clever Mercury means that, in an admirably quiet kind of way, their voice gets heard through what they do rather than what they say.

Virgo is a gentle sort of human being. They are subtle yet sensual and sensitive to their environment, and would be hard-pressed to hurt a fly. Virgo people also have a lovely, often vulnerable, appearance and they are about as refined and courteous as they come—judging by appearances at least. Deep down, though, they can be downright uptight and full of churning emotion, but what would happen if they didn't keep their cool? The world would be a much more chaotic, restless, and disorganized place!

CAREER & MONEY

Virgos are serious and conscientious workers, who are very keen to help out with things. Much of their passion and pride is derived from their job. With their highly developed analytical mind, they are superior problem-solvers and vital members of any team. Although other people sometimes find their exactness a little nerve-racking, it's only because most of them could never live up to the high standard that Virgos expect of themselves and of others—it would be better to have a Virgo as an employee than an employer! They are tireless and capable of working long hours, like a slave, but just as capable of becoming a slave-driver. If they get a bee in their bonnet about the way something should be done, they won't stop nagging until it's done right, and of course, they're never wrong. If you're someone who likes to cut corners, you couldn't possibly match Virgo's expectations.

Virgo people are adaptable, but they make particularly good analysts, accountants, scientists, craftsmen, librarians, and private secretaries. They are caring and enthusiastic as well as knowledgeable about the human body. They are very much tuned into people's needs and seem to have a sixth sense for matters concerning health, which makes them excellent care workers.

Virgos are usually working, even during their leisure time. They'll spend any spare moments on their hobbies or making things right about the house. If they were paid for every hour they worked, they'd no doubt earn more than any other sign of the zodiac. However, they aren't the most ambitious sign. If they like what they do and are good at it, they'll simply keep at it and not bother about climbing the ranks. Of course, they'll take a promotion when it's offered and when they know they're up to it, but they're more concerned with having the most suitable person for the job. If they don't feel it's them, then they'll be the first to encourage the right person.

When it comes to money, Virgo saves for a rainy day and will never be caught unawares. They handle money well, whether it's their own or someone else's, and since they're good at analyzing numbers, they're capable of making accurate forecasts and of budgeting and planning ahead. They're not cheap when they're out buying presents; in fact, they're very thoughtful and just love people. Virgo is an honorable, steadfast worker with reasonable aims. They reach the modest goals they set and are rarely without work. They do well in the world and the world is definitely a better place with Virgo around.

THE VİRGO **CHİLD**

From very early on, the Virgo child shows a need for a comforting routine. They feel most secure when they are fed, dressed, bathed, and put to bed according to an unchanging schedule. Sweet-natured and quizzical, they are alert and active with a tendency to fidget. They remain calm provided they aren't exposed to sudden loud noises or unexpected disruption. They have a finely tuned, nervous disposition and lightning-fast reflexes, but until they develop the physical agility for which they are famous, they will tend toward caution and won't be overly adventurous.

Their inquiring mind is attracted to toys and activities that require a certain amount of interaction, such as puzzles, building blocks, and picture books. They're particularly fond of gathering things from the garden—leaves, sticks, soil, and the like—and mixing them up into potions and mud pies. Little Virgos soon take on the role of organizing their physical environment by arranging their personal belongings in a way that suits them, even if that means in separate piles spaced purposely across the floor, but it's often the Virgo who will tidy away their toys without needing to be asked.

When they're playing with other children they can at first be a little serious and self-contained, but once they've made a connection and have one or two reliable, trustworthy pals, they'll blossom into lively, playful, mischievous, and energetic friends. As they grow into adolescence, they become more sensitive to criticism. Their often hidden but painful self-criticism can be their own worst enemy. It's very important that they build

self-confidence in order to feel relaxed and tolerant of their own and of others' imperfections. That is often why the teenage Virgo will develop very specialized skills in just one or two particular activities in which they can excel.

A restless, analytical mind and modest, unassuming character make the young Virgo an interesting and very pleasant person to have around.

PERFECT **GIFTS**

Typical Virgos are not really hard to please when it comes to gifts, even though they are real sticklers in other areas of life. The fact is that, when they get given a present, they receive it gracefully and with gratitude, which makes most people want to please them even more. Because they are so organized, they would appreciate a desk accessory, an organizer, a blank journal, or a diary.

Since Virgo is ruled by Mercury, they love information, so they will always appreciate a book, but not any old one. They particularly enjoy reference books full of lists. They are also into health, so any book related to diet, exercise, healing, vitamins and minerals, fitness of mind and body, or any other feel-good subject would make compelling reading for them. They would also make use of an exercise machine or simple yoga mat.

When it comes to clothing and apparel, Virgos love belts, sashes, and hip-length garments. They tend to like earthy colors, but also adore the feel and smell of unbleached pure cotton. They are also lovers of plants but if they don't have a garden, they would welcome a gift of a window box or terrarium.

FAVORITE **FOODS**

When it comes to food and drink, Virgo is as much a creature of habit as in all other areas of life. They know what they like and they'll tend to stick to it, so they'll be very cautious when it comes to trying something new. They'll usually taste just the tiniest morsel before committing themselves to a whole portion and, more frequently, they'll reject it altogether. They can be incredibly fussy not just in what they'll eat, but in its method of preparation and the way it's served, too. Unless they've been brought up to enjoy complicated dishes, their preference is toward simple food, neatly served. They don't appreciate food that looks as if it's simply been thrown on the plate, and they don't like foods that are jumbled up together. They really prefer to enjoy all the separate flavors of a meal, otherwise, in their way of thinking, the food has been "contaminated."

Nutrition is paramount to Virgos and they'll make a concerted effort to ensure that they eat a balanced diet that includes all the necessary food groups. They like a routine of breakfast, lunch, and dinner but since they're bursting with natural nervous energy, they can often be found grabbing a healthy snack— fresh fruit, nuts and seeds, or an organic cereal bar—on the run between meals.

Their favorite meals might include grilled or barbecued chicken or fish, steamed rice and vegetables, or spaghetti served with a simple sauce and salad. They can be rather choosy with dessert; they're unlikely to go for a rich, heavy pudding covered in custard. A delicate sorbet or simple chocolate mousse is more to their taste—but hold the whipped cream!

FASHION & **STYLE**

Virgos have a sophisticated but conservative dress sense. They'll often wear a simply tailored outfit with some small detail that provides a talking point. However, Virgo is one of the Earth signs so its women, particularly, are not averse to revealing some skin—though they'll do so in a classic and alluring manner, not in an overtly sexual or flashy one.

Virgos can spend hours picking their appearance apart in the mirror, yet they have a natural ability for knowing what accessories work with which outfit, and also for instinctively choosing the right outfit for every occasion. It would be a rare Virgo that ever developed "fashion-victim" tendencies; they are far too discerning to slavishly follow the latest fashion craze. They may, however, become attached to a particular clothes designer or may habitually visit the fashion shops where they have previously bought things they appreciate.

Virgo likes the colors of the forest—woody browns, leafy greens, and all the berry shades will flatter and appeal to them, as will smartly conservative navy blue. The most virginal color is, of course, pure white, but they are unlikely to choose it often; they are such neatness freaks that the way it shows up the slightest dirty mark will drive them crazy.

IDEAL HOMES

The Virgo home consists mainly of clean, unbroken lines. They don't like fuss and frills, or anything that doesn't really serve a purpose. Everything has its place and their homes are the epitome of order. Since Virgo people can often be highly strung, they need a clutter-free environment to help them keep a sense of order. There may be some Virgos who hoard things and whose homes are a mess, but they are in the minority. The moment these Virgos come across someone who is more messy than they are, they'll immediately see the logic in keeping a tidy home and will understand how much more efficiently such a home can be run. Then they'll transform themselves overnight from messy to maniacally tidy. If their neat streak is not immediately apparent, check their drawers and linen cupboards—they'll look like a perfectly laid-out shop display.

Most Virgo homes are modest and comfortable and, with Virgos being such kindly souls, they want people to feel at ease. However, the home of an extreme Virgo is so picture-perfect and immaculate that it's impossible to feel relaxed enough to sit down anywhere with a drink, except perhaps in the backyard!

RISING SIGNS

WHAT IS A **RISING** SIGN?

Your rising sign is the zodiacal sign that could be seen rising on the eastern horizon at the time and place of your birth. Each sign takes about two and a half hours to rise — approximately one degree every four minutes. Because it is so fast moving, the rising sign represents a very personal part of the horoscope, so even if two people were born on the same day and year as one another, their different rising signs will make them very different people.

It is easier to understand the rising sign when the entire birth chart is seen as a circular map of the heavens. Imagine the rising sign — or ascendant — at the eastern point of the circle. Opposite is where the Sun sets — the descendant. The top of the chart is the part of the sky that is above, where the Sun reaches at midday, and the bottom of the chart is below, where the Sun would be at midnight. These four points divide the circle, or birth chart, into four. Those quadrants are then each divided into three, making a total of twelve, known as houses, each of which represents a certain aspect of life. Your rising sign corresponds to the first house and establishes which sign of the zodiac occupied each of the other eleven houses when you were born.

All of which makes people astrologically different from one another; not all Virgos are alike! The rising sign generally indicates what a person looks like. For instance, people with Leo, the sign of kings, rising, probably walk with

a noble air and find that people often treat them like royalty. Those that have Pisces rising frequently have soft and sensitive looks and they might find that people are forever pouring their hearts out to them.

The rising sign is a very important part of the entire birth chart and should be considered in combination with the Sun sign and all the other planets!

THE RiSiNG SiGNS FOR ViRGO

To work out your rising sign, you need to know your exact time of birth— if hospital records aren't available, try asking your family and friends. Now turn to the charts on pages 38–43. There are three charts, covering New York, Sydney, and London, all set to Greenwich Mean Time. Choose the correct chart for your place of birth and, if necessary, add or subtract the number of hours difference from GMT (for example, Sydney is approximately ten hours ahead, so you need to subtract ten hours from your time of birth). Then use a ruler to carefully find the point where your GMT time of birth meets your date of birth—this point indicates your rising sign.

ViRGO WiTH **ARiES** RiSiNG

When Aries is rising the result is a bold and enterprising individual. This rising sign produces a questing mind with a hunger for knowledge—a knowledge that can be developed into sound understanding and can eventually be translated into fine, highly skilled physical activity. Virgo

people with Aries rising embrace this process wholeheartedly. Virgo already has an abundance of nervous energy and when it's combined with the enthusiasm of Aries, then there's no room left for the shy, retiring expression of their sign, so much so that they will often surprise themselves with an act of courage—for example, asking a complete stranger out on a date! But when it comes to work, no job is too great for the Virgo with Aries rising. They're not afraid of getting their hands dirty, as long as there's some running water and a bottle of antibacterial soap nearby. They're industrious and will throw themselves into life with verve and vigor. Bright and cheerful, they help others out whenever they can and they provide happy, healing energy for all those in their company.

VIRGO WITH **TAURUS** RISING

Kind, caring, and generous, the Virgo with Taurus rising appears to be calm, relaxed, and totally at ease, but on the inside they're bursting with ideas and energy that are looking for expression and a creative outlet. These are some of the most skilled artisans of all the Virgos; when combined with Venus-ruled Taurus, their love and appreciation of all physical representations of beauty is heightened, as is their desire to become a conscientious creator of wonderful, sensually alluring *objets d'art*. They have an eye for what is pleasing and attractive and they're not afraid to explore their imagination and express what they find there with stunning impact. Because they have such reverence for all that is born out of the magic of the

universe, they enjoy the company of children and make great teachers. They are patient and quick to interpret the needs of a child and, under their influence, a child can blossom and produce their creative best. Once their own interest has been engaged, Virgos with Taurus rising will be highly productive and will express themselves in a unique manner.

VIRGO WITH **GEMINI** RISING

This is the ultimate "virgin intellectual;" they embody both a lively and innocent thirst for information and a mature skill in applying the knowledge gained to build a sound future. Although they are fun, energetic, and very chatty, they tend to hide their light under a bushel in the backyard, where the fence might be a favorite spot to gossip with the neighbor! They can appear totally free and independent yet they often prefer to stay in their own familiar surroundings or with a trusted group of friends who cherish and adore them for their brilliant conversation and quick wit. The Virgo with Gemini rising is someone who inherits a family legacy or some family trait. When young, they may be anxious to show that they are not at all like their forefathers; they'll assert their individuality, but as they grow, they learn to appreciate what they've gained from others. Their family foundation often provides them with a strong base—a confidence that they carry with them wherever they go. Within the family, whether blood relatives or the family of friends, they will be the person that everyone goes to for cheering up or for help in solving problems.

VIRGO WITH **CANCER** RISING

The emotional sensitivity that Cancer rising lends to the Virgo character makes for a truly sweet and unassuming person with an instinctive ability to express things that are often difficult to put into words. They are incredibly receptive to the vibes around them, so even though they can appear quiet, serious, and perhaps even a little nervous, it's because they're constantly absorbing every detail of their environment, which they are then able to communicate eloquently to others. The Virgo with Cancer rising is a moving and convincing storyteller, and therefore makes a great teacher and orator. They speak clearly and concisely and their way of conveying an idea can be mesmerizingly persuasive. Yet they are sincere and earnest individuals. They have a strong need to belong and are fiercely protective of family and friends. They are also naturally caring and nurturing; no one who comes to them for support or assistance would ever be turned away. Added to all this is a shrewd and clever ability in business and all things mercantile. Their protective instincts will extend to offering financial support to those they know and love. They care deeply but they're no one's fool.

VIRGO WITH **LEO** RISING

Showmanship and the skill to back it up is what the Virgo native has when Leo is the rising sign. Whether they choose theater work in the literal sense is unimportant; what's certain is that they'll have a fine ability for

making everything they do theatrical. From top to toe, these people dress and behave in order to impress; they have excellent taste and an elegance of manner that is beyond reproach. Their secret fear is that someone will find reason to criticize them, so they work doubly hard not only in their strict attention to detail in the duties and services they perform, but also on their image and appearance. The Virgo with Leo rising sets great store on the material world but, as they grow, they realize that their gold is to be found inside their heart. They stand tall and proud, a picture of elegance, prestige, and perfection. They're popular and not easy to get to know because everyone else seems to want to know them. Those who do manage to get close will enjoy their staunch trust and loyalty.

VIRGO WITH **VIRGO** RISING

♍ The Virgo with Virgo rising is a consistent self-starter. They enjoy being involved in plenty of activity; not only does it help to burn off excess nervous energy, but engaging both mentally and physically provides them with a very positive expression of their many talents. They are industrious, quick learners with a real enthusiasm for new experiences. In time, they build up a large cache of skills that they can apply to many different areas of life. With all this going for them it's difficult to understand why they appear so modest and even so lacking in self-confidence, but tooting their own horn is not what they're about; they let their achievements speak for themselves—and they do! They may not make a lot of noise but

they never fail to get noticed. They expect excellence and perfection from other people because that's exactly what they give, and they manage it with style and grace. Whatever project they set their hand to, they'll finish to an impeccable standard. They've got a magic touch.

VIRGO WITH **LIBRA** RISING

Virgo already has a penchant for cleanliness and order but, with Libra rising, they get an added feel for harmony and beauty. Now, not only will they organize their life so that everything is in its place at all times, but they'll add a touch of fantasy and a sense of dreamy, inviting romanticism. This will extend to their demeanor as well as to their outward appearance, where they'll apply their meticulous attention to detail. They are refined, compassionate, and idealistic, with a quiet, modest, and pleasant manner, always putting the needs of others before their own. But this doesn't always work to their best advantage. In fact, they can sometimes be their own worst enemy, suppressing their needs in favor of the needs of others. They're real people-pleasers but the lesson they must learn is to please themselves, too. The Virgo with Libra rising is a very likable human being, mentally keen, perceptive, and highly imaginative. They often have great artistic ability and may well succeed—indeed excel—in the art world. They have finely tuned senses, an understanding of the creative language of music and art, and know intuitively how to tune into their environment.

VIRGO WITH **SCORPIO** RISING

♏ With Scorpio rising, Virgo appears to be even more self-contained and reserved than usual, yet they also have a need to be involved with friends and people with a common interest. They're quick-witted, prudent, and just a touch suspicious. They're also inventive and enterprising, and can accomplish much if they try diligently to gain the necessary knowledge to bring projects to completion. They have a penetrating insight into what makes people tick and they use their natural analytical abilities to help others understand their own motivations. The desire to be of use to humanity as a whole is a powerful driving force in their life, so they'll often make time to think through the problems of the world in the hope of finding some solution. They're not easy to read and their inscrutability can often lead others into misunderstanding their intentions and motivations. They always seem to be interested in other people yet reveal very little of themselves, tending to be secretive, though for no special reason. They have amazing mental faculties, which they often put at the service of organizations whose politics they share by working as volunteers.

VIRGO WITH **SAGITTARIUS** RISING

♐ When Sagittarius is rising, Virgo's natural inclination toward physical efficiency is frequently expressed in the form of athleticism. These people tend to have well-formed bodies and long legs, which are great for

running. They have the urge to be at the top of the sporting tree, not just for the status that comes with it, but also because of their need to test the limits of systemized training on the body. Naturally, sport and the perfection of the body are not the only ways these people will express themselves; the Virgo with Sagittarius rising is ambitious and may apply that ambition to any endeavor. They also happen to be very attractive to others—perhaps not great beauties, but with a magnetic, charismatic presence. What fascinates these individuals is the application of systems, be they philosophical or concrete. They enjoy gathering together all that is needed to build something from scratch, and they will pay strict attention to the detail. Their efforts often result in success; indeed, they expect no less of themselves and they can be downright hard on themselves along the way. But not everything about them is serious or related to achievement; they are also warm, charming, fun-loving individuals.

VIRGO WITH **CAPRICORN** RISING

The Virgo with Capricorn rising is a truly earthy individual, often quiet and gentle but also industrious and self-reliant. Totally physically tuned in, they can appear serious and contemplative, as though they were absorbing into their very bones all the subtle and weighty information around them, which of course they are. They have a philosophical turn of mind and seek knowledge and understanding with patience and dignity. With time, what they discover is often applied to projects of a sound business

nature, for these Virgos are able to spot an opportunity. They'll go after it and use their determination to turn it into a great personal achievement, but they'll take their time. Even as a child, they knew how to pace themselves and, as a result, they may appear laid-back. In the fable of the turtle and the hare, they're the turtle—the one who seems to be lagging but who ends up winning in the end. As an adult, they take the same slow but sure road; this is their guarantee of success, whether they're dealing with a relationship, work, money, or planning a vacation. They are meticulous, exacting, and efficient to a tee, and are also determined yet aware of the needs of others. They may always win but, for them, it's not winning that's important; what's important is finding the right way to reach the finishing post.

VIRGO WITH **AQUARIUS** RISING

〰〰 The Virgo with Aquarius rising is a pleasant, reasonable, sympathetic individual, with just a touch of quirky eccentricity. Often highly intelligent and with an exceptional memory for details and facts, they could bury themselves in books for days in order to get right to the bottom of some piece of information or idea before they'll let it go. That's not to suggest that they're obsessive—but they certainly can be! The problem is that they simply can't do anything in half-measures. They're thorough, and have an amazing capacity for concentration. They're also pretty intuitive, which gives them that extra something that they need in order to tie up all the loose ends on a project. They're sociable and enjoy psychologically revealing conversations

with friends, and since they're also good listeners, they show quite a talent as an armchair analyst. Working professionally in this field is something that they would enjoy and would excel at too, as they have enough emotional detachment to offer rational responses. They're definitely into people and are also lucky enough to be well rewarded by them for their efforts.

VIRGO WITH **PISCES** RISING

This is the idealistic Virgo who looks only for the good in everyone they meet and who will do all they can to help to bring it out of them. With Pisces rising, they possess oceans of empathy and loving kindness and, as a result, often gather a swathe of lost souls and strays around them, all looking for the comfort and advice that they're so good at offering. They're receptive, hospitable, and truly needed, and they're very content with that state of affairs. It's true that they'll sometimes be taken advantage of, but it's equally true that they'll often inspire a fierce devotion in those whose lives they have touched. If they had a dime for every lost soul who'd come to them for sympathy, then they'd be wealthy by middle age. Although they may not always seem so from the outside, they're sensitive and they absorb vibes like a sponge, so they need to make a conscious effort to shield themselves from the harshness of the world. Luckily, as well as their waifs and strays, the Virgo with Pisces rising also has at least one devoted person nearby to save their day.

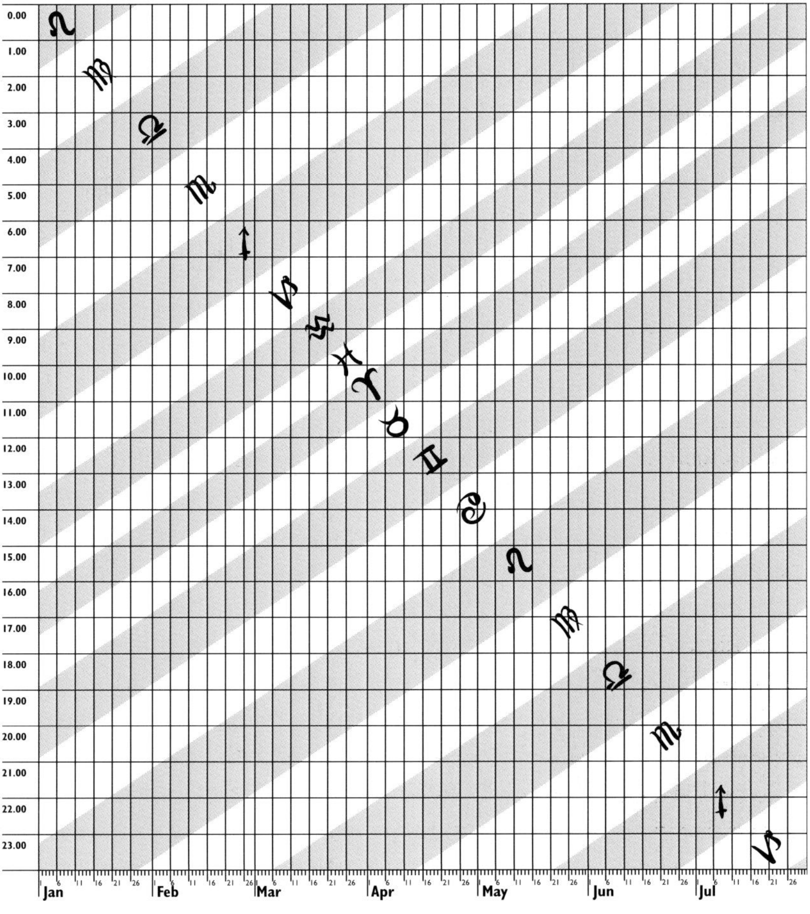
0.00
1.00
2.00
3.00
4.00
5.00
6.00
7.00
8.00
9.00
10.00
11.00
12.00
13.00
14.00
15.00
16.00
17.00
18.00
19.00
20.00
21.00
22.00
23.00
Jan
Feb
Mar
Apr
May
Jun
Jul

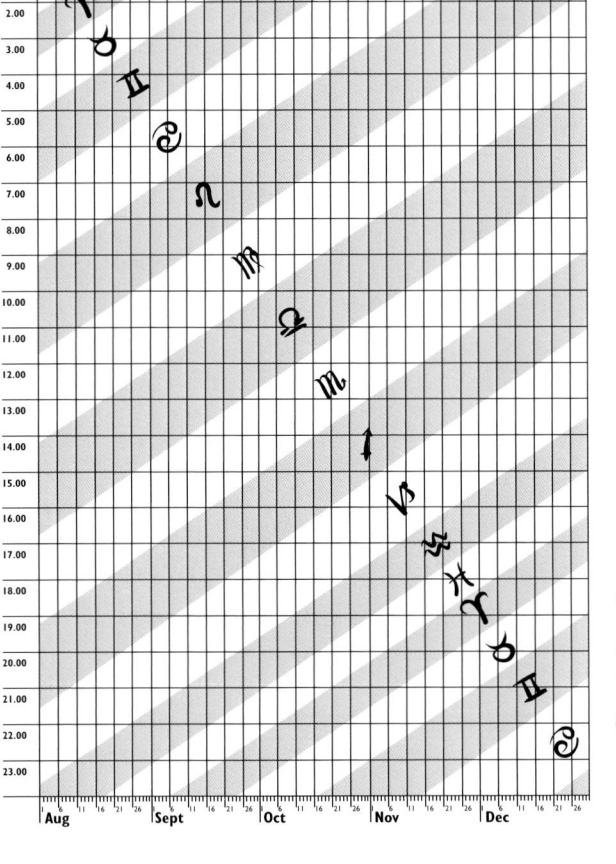

RISING SIGN
CHART

New York

latitude 39N00
meridian 75W00

♈ aries		♎ libra	
♉ taurus		♏ scorpio	
♊ gemini		♐ sagittarius	
♋ cancer		♑ capricorn	
♌ leo		♒ aquarius	
♍ virgo		♓ pisces	

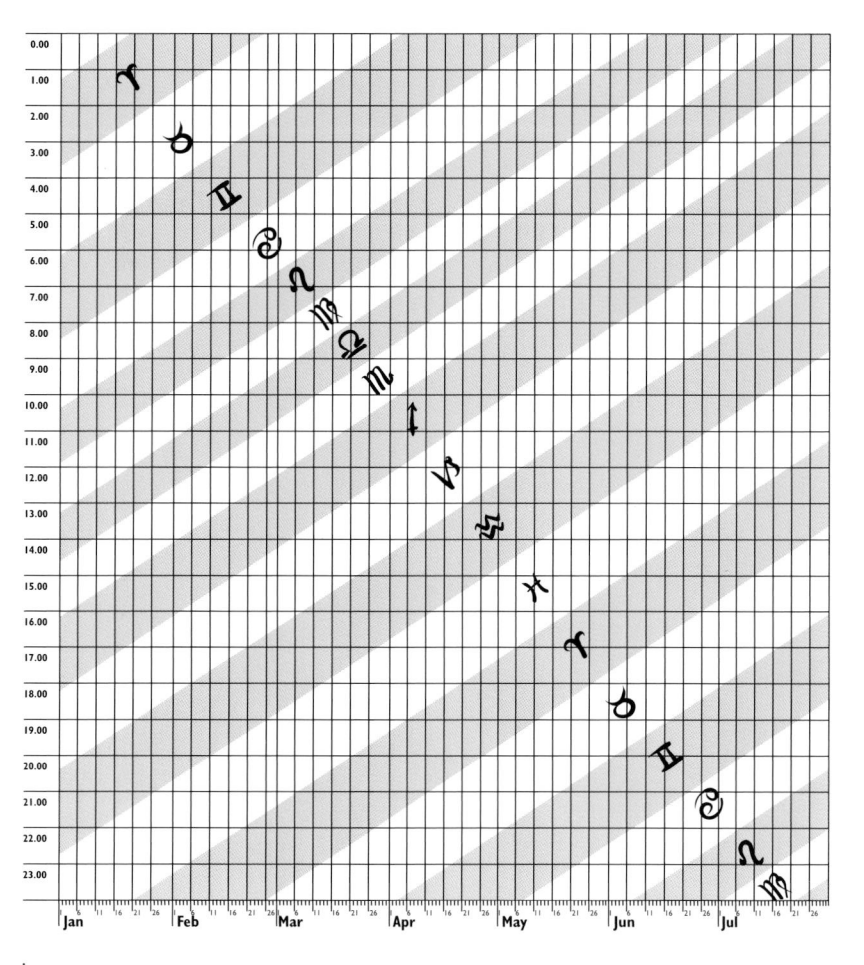

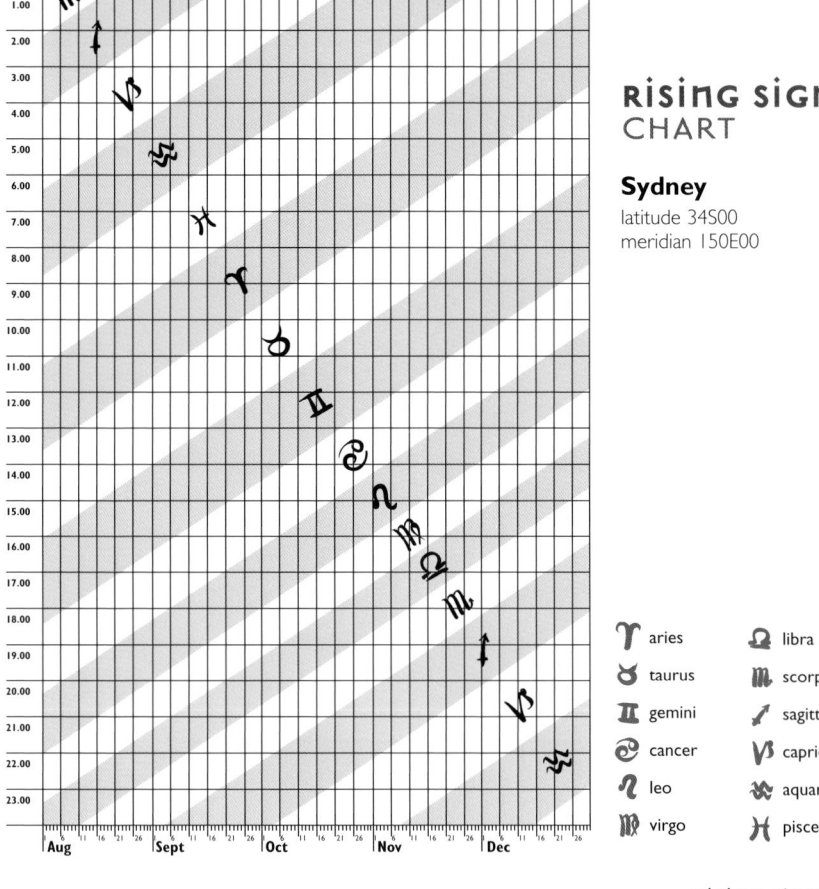

RISING SIGN
CHART

Sydney
latitude 34S00
meridian 150E00

♈	aries	♎	libra
♉	taurus	♏	scorpio
♊	gemini	♐	sagittarius
♋	cancer	♑	capricorn
♌	leo	♒	aquarius
♍	virgo	♓	pisces

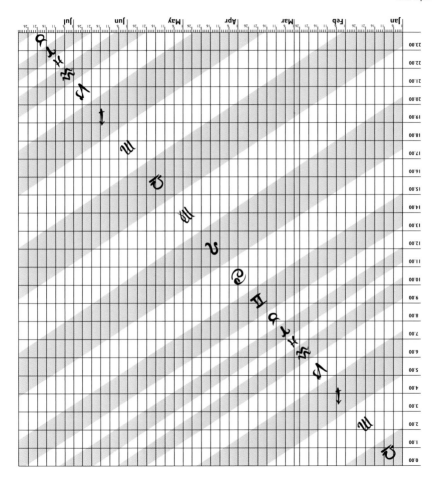

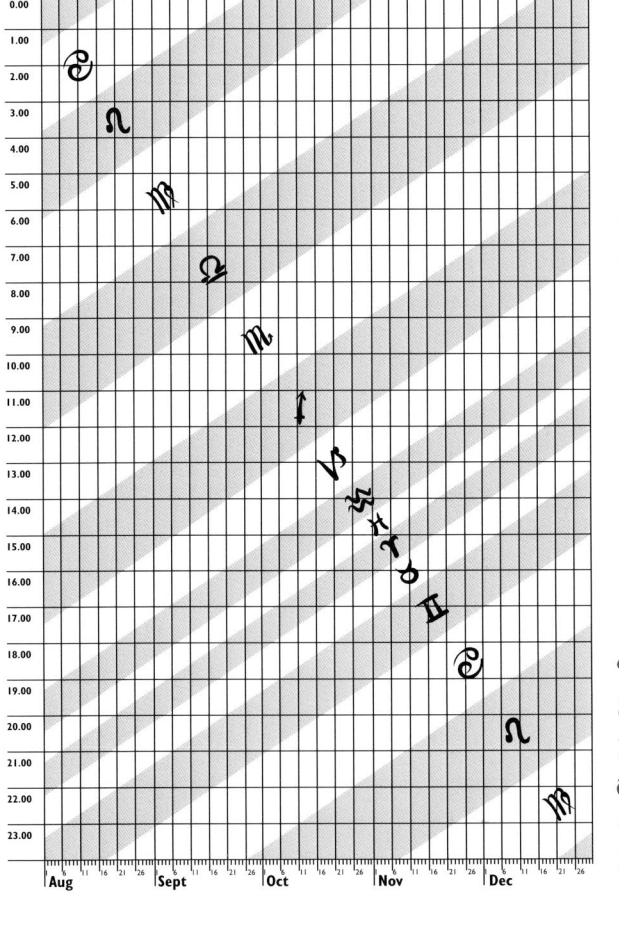

RISING SIGN
CHART

London
latitude 51N30
meridian 0W00

♈ aries   ♎ libra

♉ taurus   ♏ scorpio

♊ gemini   ♐ sagittarius

♋ cancer   ♑ capricorn

♌ leo   ♒ aquarius

♍ virgo   ♓ pisces

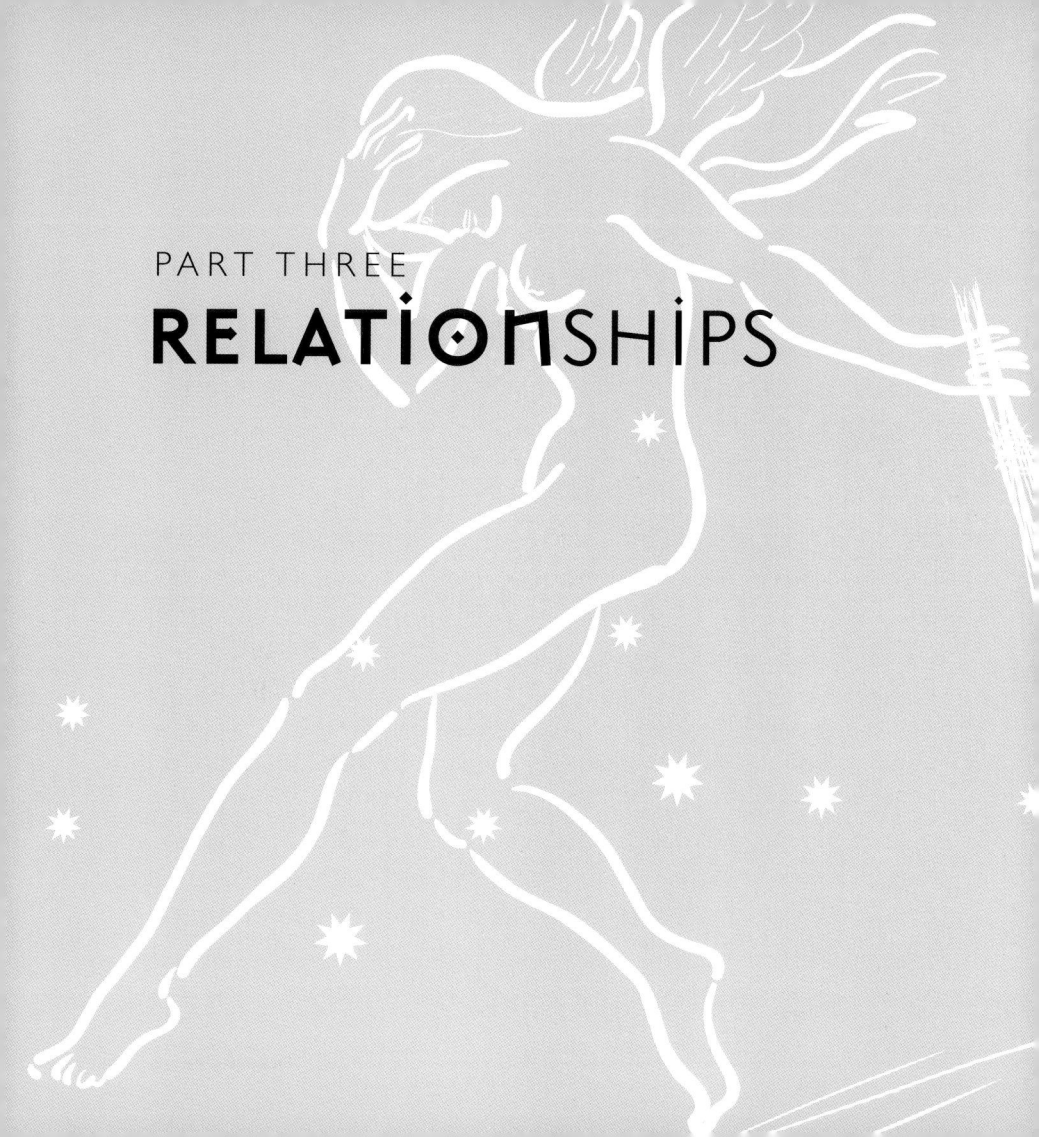

PART THREE
RELATIONSHIPS

THE VIRGO **FRIEND**

Because they can be a little shy about coming forward, Virgos won't push themselves onto others. They prefer to hang back and wait to be invited to engage in conversation, but once they have been invited, and provided the topic under discussion is something that they have some knowledge of, they will quickly demonstrate their talent for stimulating communication. They are attentive listeners and are fascinated by the idiosyncrasies of others, so it doesn't take long for them to become part of a regular group. It's at this point that Virgos really get into their stride; once they're on familiar ground and sharing common interests, they become confident and relaxed, and they'll unleash their insightful, lively wit for the benefit and amusement of others.

They say a friend in need is a friend indeed, and this perfectly describes the naturally helpful Virgo, who is frequently found offering support to friends. This can sometimes lead to Virgo being taken advantage of. But if the friendship is built on mutual trust and respect then nobody will be better able or more willing to sort out a practical problem than a Virgo.

When they're out on the town with their pals, Virgos may not be the ones instigating high jinks or indulging in wild behavior, but neither will they be killjoys. They'll go along for the ride and will be happy to provide the quick, clever commentary that will add to everyone's fun and enjoyment.

VIRGO WITH **ARIES**

It's difficult for Aries and Virgo to see eye to eye. For the most part, they're running at different speeds. Arians wants to get where they're going fast, paying little attention to the finer details. Those finer details, however, are what intrigues Virgo so much — the intricate subtleties of organization and efficiency, practice and preparation. One has no patience at all; the other has the patience of a saint. Inevitably there will be points where they meet — their mutual respect for one thing — but even when they like each other and are fully engaged in some mutual interest, they'll find this friendship incredibly hard work.

VIRGO WITH **TAURUS**

Being a Mercurial sign, Virgo, with its witty remarks, insightfulness, and ability to reason things through with precision, will never fail to hold the Bull's interest. Taurus, meanwhile, offers unwavering calm and loyal and steadfast support that can soothe and calm Virgo friends whenever they are nervous or on edge. However, Taureans don't enjoy having their Virgo friends over-analyze their psychology, and their famous stubbornness is very limiting to Virgo's quick and nimble mind. However, as both signs are of the Earth element, there is a good rapport between them and the relationship flows easily, with each having a very grounded and natural understanding of the other.

VIRGO WITH GEMINI

This is a strange combination in the friendship stakes. They share some common ground and both offer something that the other does not have, yet there is a random quality to their relationship. Mental connection happens easily enough and their conversations are bound to be stimulating, fun, and interesting, but Gemini can lose patience with a Virgo who wants to slow communication down and analyze things more deeply, while Virgo may find the way Gemini constantly changes perspective to be flippant and childish. They'll both enjoy spending time with each other but they're unlikely to be joined at the hip.

VIRGO WITH CANCER

Cancer and Virgo both have an innate gentleness about them, so as friends they get on very well together and will often choose similar things to do. Virgo seems able to contain the sometimes strong emotions of Cancer, while Cancer will encourage Virgo to take more initiative. This friendship will continue to grow because while they have a different perspective on life, their sense of humor dovetails and they'll find that they enjoy many private jokes together. As a result, they'll feel as if they belong to some kind of exclusive club whose members enjoy plenty of wry amusement and raucous laughter.

VIRGO WITH **LEO**

♌ This relationship has friendship potential only if the two of them stay true to certain aspects of their nature. For the Leo, it is always to be warm and generous, while for the Virgo it is to be helpful and of service. If the Leo, however much admired by the Virgo, becomes capricious and demanding, or the Virgo, however much respected by the Leo, becomes critical and pedantic, then the friendship could be a little harder to maintain. If they're part of a group of friends, then these two may hardly ever see one another, but with just the two together, they'll make great buddies. Both will feel safe knowing that they can rely on one another through thick and thin.

VIRGO WITH **VIRGO**

♍ There is an immediate sense of connection between two Virgos. Both are so mentally and physically attuned to one another's presence that a knowing bond develops without them actually having to say anything. Having such a bond is fine, but if they don't actually speak up, then how are they going to enjoy the deep and meaningful insights that the other has to offer? Somehow, they manage. It was probably a Virgo who coined the phrase "Actions speak louder than words." When they're together, they're always busy and never at a loss for something to do. They make an incredibly industrious team—too good for words, in fact.

ViRGO WiTH **LiBRA**

There are certain sensibilities that these two share that make them natural friends. Virgo's need for order and Libra's need for harmony somehow dovetail to ensure an easy flow of thoughts and deeds between them. These two could happily spend hours together sitting over lunch and picking apart all sorts of ideas, or meeting up regularly to go to dance, yoga, or meditation classes. They don't need to go home together to experience the other's individual quirks and idiosyncrasies; they're more than happy developing an easygoing friendship based on a weekly get-together.

ViRGO WiTH **SCORPiO**

On the surface, these two seem so very different; Scorpio has a deep, emotional approach to life and Virgo has a subtle, physical one. And yet they share some similarities and compatibilities, which they instinctively recognize in each other and which make it easy for a friendship to blossom between them. They have a way of affirming the other's worth through their natural acceptance of and agreement with the other. Both are, to some extent, detectives, the one discovering the emotional side of things and the other the physical, so what they learn separately then feeds the other's desire for greater understanding. They may eventually come to rely on each other simply for emotional support; this will ensure a special kind of connection between them.

ViRGO WiTH **SAGiTTARiUS**

This is a quizzical friendship that may take a while to develop. Both will find the other interesting and pleasant enough, but they won't necessarily arrange to get together again unless they share a common hobby or interest. If they do, then repeated exposure to one another will mean that they gain a great deal from the other's special talent or particular perspective. They have much to offer one another but it will take some time for them to recognize this fact. Once they do, then they will make plans to meet up, but this will be for a dose of interesting information rather than for some company.

ViRGO WiTH **CAPRiCORN**

This is such an easy alliance—which is why Virgo and Capricorn become allies. Even on those rare occasions when they're not together, they're on each other's minds and should anyone have a harsh word to say about the other, they won't hesitate to stand up for them. These two will hang out together and will totally get where the other is coming from. In fact, with both of them so industrious, this friendship could probably develop into a creative partnership where they reap real material rewards as well as having fun together.

Virgo with **AQUARiUS**

The mental connection that these two share will allow them to enjoy hours of intellectual exploration that each will find spellbindingly stimulating. However, although mutual respect comes easily to them, a few problems could arise if Aquarius's somewhat zany ideas appear too eccentric and extreme for Virgo's final analysis. Water-Bearers want to boldly go where no mind has gone before and won't appreciate the Virgo need to ground them in reality. In short bursts, this could be a wonderfully productive duo, but coming up with ideas and plans to move forward, then stopping and starting, would be asking for trouble!

Virgo with **PiSCES**

These are both thoughtful, gentle people who will find that they have much in common. Although their perspectives are diametrically opposed—Virgo is concerned with organization and understanding in the physical realm, and Pisces with ultimate freedom in the emotional and spiritual realms—both are flexible enough to make space for their interests to align and to establish a mutually fascinating friendship. In fact, their individual extremes might even begin to rub off on one another, which will bring them both a better balance between chaos and order. Virgo and Pisces have a natural affinity and affection for one another; this will mean a lifelong link.

THE **ViRGO WOMAN** iN LOVE

The Virgo woman in love doesn't gush, nor does she buy cutesy cards covered in fluffy pink hearts and teddy bears to send to her lover. She won't flutter her eyelashes or leave baby-talk messages on his answering machine, and yet, after her own fashion, she can be very demonstrative when it comes to showing her love. Usually, though, her way will take a form that many men won't recognize, for this lady is rather complex. She shows her love by giving her lover respect, by being available to sit down and talk to him, by offering advice or assistance in solving his problems, and by discussing with him how he can make the most of his good points.

Does that mean that she's harsh and unlovely? Not a bit! She's extremely sweet, very attentive to his needs, and usually a pretty good cook with a fine repertoire of dishes that will be great for his health. Although the domestic goddess role is one that she can adopt with mind-boggling efficiency, she would resent any man who tried to keep her barefoot and pregnant in the kitchen when she has so many other skills at her fingertips that need practice to make perfect. She's incredibly capable, and a good multi-tasker. When they go on vacation, she'll help load up the car with the camping equipment, make sure that she's packed the first-aid kit and has equipped the picnic basket with caviar, champagne, and a tin-opener, and will ensure that the book her man is currently reading hasn't been left behind in the bathroom. She'll have neatly stowed her sexy new nightgown, as well as her lipstick and walking boots, and she'll have checked the oil level and the spare tire. And

she'll have done all this with her cell phone clutched to her ear while she leaves instructions for her work colleagues to follow during her absence. And all this simply so that she can spend a couple of days surrounded by nature in the arms of her lover. What bigger demonstration of her feelings does any man need?

A Virgo woman wouldn't turn her nose up at a trip to a five-star spa hotel, to be pampered and preened while drinking champagne from crystal flutes, but her true idea of romance is a quite different scenario: cuddling up by a campfire while contemplating the stars, or hiking up a hill to watch the sunset. Not for her the clichéd violins playing at the dinner table or the heart-shaped chocolates on the pillow. And like all the Earth signs, she's an incredibly physical, sexy lover. Sensuality is her thing—the very word makes her tingle with delight. But she requires trust and respect from her partner, as well as a powerful display of his passionate sexual need for her if she is to reach the white-hot heat of her eroticism. This girl needs to be needed; in fact, she loves to be needed!

VIRGO WOMAN WITH **ARIES MAN**

In love: All the fire, energy, and confidence that are so apparent in the Aries man are a complete turn-on for the composed and cool Virgo lady. He gives her a real charge, whether they're out painting the town red or holed up at home together. He finds her demure femininity highly arousing, feeling drawn to her because she can be so cool. He desperately wants her approval but somehow, she never quite feels inclined to give it to him completely. She has an incredible ability to put his life in order—not that it will be appreciated. In fact, it's something he might resent, except when it comes to once more being able to find things he thought were lost. She'll need to be watchful for when this Ram charges with anger: he'll leave her in a crumpled heap. Much to his dismay, unless he offers a heartfelt apology, it will take her quite a while to pick herself up off the floor, and when she does, he'll be made to feel guilty. Not a sensation that the Aries man enjoys. She'll withdraw her usual selfless support and will feel completely justified in allowing the critical side of her nature to be focused solely on him. It will be extremely hard work for the Aries man to get back in the good books of this graceful lady. If she doesn't learn to forgive and forget, he might soon decide that this relationship is too big a job for him to handle.

In bed: The sexual allure of the demure Virgo woman is quite irresistible to the Aries man, who is the kind of enthusiastic lover that will have her panting for more. Yet for all his sexual energy

and powers of enticement, somehow he only manages to scratch the surface of her well-contained sexual desires. His lust for immediate and spontaneous sexual gratification doesn't often meet with this lady's approval. She can be happy with a quickie on occasion, but more often than not she wants to see diligence and dedication in her lover. He may be up for doing it more than once, but for her that means endlessly going back to the beginning and starting all over again. It's fabulous for the figure to get a good physical workout, but just as she's warmed up and ready for the really hard stuff, he's headed for the shower and a cup of coffee! That's not to say that this sexual relationship can't work, only that it *is* work — for both of them. With the right man, the Virgo woman is sensual and earthy, and she loves to make love but there also has to be loyalty and a genuine exchange of deep feelings, both of which the Aries man might offer. At worst, a Virgo woman can stick at an unsatisfactory relationship for only so long and an Aries man, not at all. At best, as they are quick learners, they'll be keen to learn about one another. If they can teach one another to stick around, they'll both enjoy plenty of pleasure!

VİRGO WOMAN WİTH **TAURUS MAN**

 **In love:** It may take a while for the Taurus man to get under the skin of the reticent Virgo woman, but when he does, it's in such a pleasant way. Neither of these two Earth signs are quick to fall in love, but once they do, they both tend to remain true. He's persistent and

if he has his heart set on her, he'll pursue her until she submits. However, her very feminine qualities should not be mistaken for signs of weakness. On the contrary, she is actually a rather discerning character and she will not be persuaded to do anything unless she feels deep down inside that she wants to do it. If he gives her time, he'll earn her trust gradually, with his charm and utter determination. He'll know he has won her over, not just from the words she speaks, but from the feeling that she's truly given her heart to him. The Taurus man's caring and purposeful nature will go a long way to helping his Virgo woman to forget about his less attractive characteristics—his stubbornness and pedantry, for example—just as her efficiency, good taste, and subtlety will allay any fears he has about her being highly strung and fussy. And while he doesn't take well to her need to analyze every tiny aspect of his character, he senses her hidden depths and passions and so he is happy to indulge her occasionally. The Virgo woman is easily seduced by the Taurus man, who is so full of romantic gestures and sensual affection, and she values his calm, powerful presence, especially when she's feeling nervous and unsure of herself.

In bed: If there was one man a Virgo woman might be willing to jump into bed with straight away, it would be a Taurus man. This is a match that both will instinctively know is going to create fireworks in their otherwise ordinary and down-to-earth lives. It's one relationship that will certainly ruffle a few sheets! Since a Taurus man is so very determined in the pursuit of his hedonistic pleasures, it's no surprise

that sex comes top of his list, particularly sex with a Virgo woman. He'll work very hard to learn where her erogenous zones are and will know instinctively just what to do with them once he's found them. What is more, he won't mind if it takes her a while to get with the program. This man enjoys his studies very much! It's these important little details that the Virgo woman really appreciates. She might act the hard task master, insisting that practice makes perfect, but, with her immediate response to every correctly placed touch, she also makes his job easy. It's true that the male Bull is rough, ready, and a little crude when he's feeling horny—which Bulls generally are—while the demure and modest Virgo lady is apparently more refined, but it should be remembered that she is as earthy as he is and she is just as capable of mucking in when there is deliciously dirty work to be done (though she'll be the first to head for the shower afterwards). This is marathon lovemaking at its very best!

VIRGO WOMAN WITH GEMINI MAN

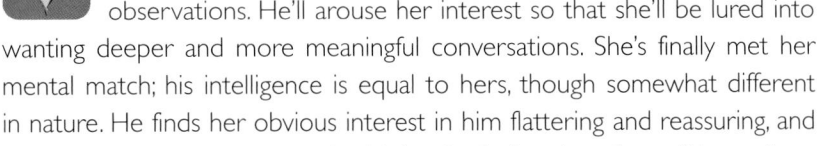

In love: Conversations with a Gemini man give the Virgo woman a real buzz; she'll be impressed by his rhetoric and clever observations. He'll arouse her interest so that she'll be lured into wanting deeper and more meaningful conversations. She's finally met her mental match; his intelligence is equal to hers, though somewhat different in nature. He finds her obvious interest in him flattering and reassuring, and if the two of them can maintain this level of adoration, that will keep them

going. But while the two of them are, mentally speaking, busy little bees, he has a tendency to show off, buzzing about from one subject to another and perhaps becoming as irritating as a wasp. And he can be just like that in the love department, too—all buzz and no substance! Though laughter should flow easily between these two individuals, she'll never quite get him to explore the emotional side of their relationship with the depth that she desires. For the Gemini man, conversations that cater to a Virgo woman's need for everything to be analyzed in minute detail are like sticky fly paper. They only serve to make him frantic to pursue his freedom, which has the effect of making her jittery. With all that nervous energy bouncing back and forth between them, the relationship won't feel very comfortable. Unless they're both willing to work at this relationship, once they've flitted, fluttered, and buzzed around each other for a while, it won't be long before one of them just buzzes off permanently.

In bed: Because she is totally into his sense of humor and she is highly attracted to the quick and easy way that he communicates, the Gemini man could lure the Virgo woman giggling all the way to the bedroom. Laughter is a powerful aphrodisiac and when these two get together, it just seems so natural. He fascinates her and encourages her sexual urges so that all she wants to do is to get to know him more and more intimately. However, once they're lying side by side and are ready for some loving, he doesn't quite know what to do with her. Perhaps he'll whisper some sweet and seductive fantasies in her ear and tease her a little,

and then she might do the same for him! They each have a very similar seduction technique for getting the other into bed and, predictably, this could get a little boring for the Gemini man, which means that the Virgo lady will once again find her man lacking in substance. In the end, for her at least, these fantasies only work when there's a bit of flesh attached to them. The Gemini man will definitely connect mentally with his Virgo lover, but on a physical level the bits don't always fit so smoothly. However, both do have a brilliant capacity for creativity and they could easily arouse one another's sexual appetite by introducing an element of surprise. If the love is there, the drive to make a more meaningful physical relationship will be there, too. Together these two could forge a strong love that will sustain many erotic nights of passion.

VIRGO WOMAN WITH CANCER MAN

In love: It's possible for the Virgo lady to scare the sensitive Crab away by sending out vibes that make her seem untouchable, but he's good for her and if she realizes it, she won't let him scuttle out of her life that quickly. She only has to switch on her soft, alluring charm to make him stay long enough to get to know her a little better. And the more time he spends with her, the more he'll desire her! The Cancer man loves earthy women with a twist, which is exactly what she is, and he's the one who could finally melt her resolve to remain unattached. The Virgo lady needs a man she can really trust, and she'll certainly find one in the loyal

and loving Cancer man: a Crab in love makes the most sensitive, caring, and protective partner imaginable. What's more, these two will spend a lot of time together laughing, or at least being highly amused. The only difficulty may lie in the Virgo woman's tendency to criticize. The Cancer man doesn't take criticism well at all and he may sulk for days without telling her why. She needs to give him lots of praise and a good place for her to start is in the area of his ambition. That's one of the aspects of his character that she finds most appealing. His money-making schemes provide her with the opportunity to show off her wonderful organizational talents; together they could make a formidable team. Seeing the fruits of their labors will inspire the love they share to grow.

 **In bed:** Both of these individuals are very caring with those they love, and as long as they can keep this caring on the physical, as well as the emotional level, their love will stay alive forever. The Virgo woman and Cancer man have a fresh, friendly approach to intimacy and they naturally accept and understand the unspoken side of the other's erotic desires. When she gets into a lovemaking frame of mind, the Virgo lady has a delightfully skillful touch. She loves to look after her man's bodily needs just as much as he likes to caress her emotionally and physically. He'll know how to open up her feelings for him by pushing all the right buttons and she'll instinctively make that earthy physical connection with him. Her demure, butter-wouldn't-melt-in-the-mouth exterior will come tumbling down to expose a fierce sexuality. Their lovemaking is perfectly

matched; however, they can both be shy at first, so their relationship will need time to develop. Give them years together and their lovemaking will mature into something very beautiful, long after most people are well past their expiration date.

VIRGO WOMAN WITH LEO MAN

In love: A rather curious thing happens to the Virgo woman when she comes face to face with the male Lion; her usually nervous temperament is oddly calmed. His strength and warmth overwhelm her with feelings of comfort and well-being. She can see all his unique qualities for what they are and she finds his idiosyncrasies appealing and totally fascinating. The limelight-loving Lion is ideal for the Virgo woman since she prefers a partner who can shine while she remains slightly apart, happily observing from the sidelines. Meanwhile, she completely intrigues him; the Leo man appreciates her delicacy and good taste as well as her attention to detail, though he may, at times, find her fondness for analyzing his behavior a strange and uncomfortable way for her to express her interest in him. He's much happier when he can simply see her adoring, unquestioning face looking up at him. If Lady Virgo is too critical—which she inevitably will be—she'll quickly discover what a super-sensitive soul this man has. However, it has to be said that the Leo man can be domineering and he is certainly no shrinking violet when it comes to defending himself against criticism. He simply won't tolerate being picked on and he will let her know

in no uncertain terms just how he feels about it. Luckily, she's adaptable and, because he always wants to be perfect, he'll do all he can to treat her right. These two work really well as a couple—they'll enjoy life together wherever they find themselves.

 **In bed:** When flesh meets flesh the Leo man really is hot property. The slightest touch of his skin ignites a burning desire within the Virgo woman and she wants to get closer and closer to the flame. However, taming the Lion could take some time, and she must take care not to get burnt in the process. She has a delectable physical appeal that brings out the hungry beast in him, so he might be a touch impatient to get started on devouring her. If she honestly shows how much she adores her Leo man, that will fire him up even more, while, if she can open herself up completely to him, she may well discover that here is the lover to bring out the hidden harlot in the Virgin. She finds the ardent way in which he expresses his sexuality to be rather a turn-on, but to really access her own white-hot passion she needs him to take control, not only of her pleasure, but of his as well. The Leo man and the Virgo woman can really get it on together simply by being their natural, raw selves—he is all man, and she is all woman. When they're out with friends and workmates, they'll walk tall because they have given each other great sexual confidence and deep inside they both know that they are the ultimate man and woman.

VIRGO WOMAN WITH **VIRGO MAN**

In love: Since these two individuals are so much alike, it's easy to see why there would be an initial attraction between the Virgo man and woman. They enjoy the banter that results from their keen wit, and when the two of them sit down to a good gossip, it can go on for hours, turning into a deep, meaningful analysis of the psychology of the human condition. And since they've finally met someone who feels the same way they do about things, such as hygiene issues, for example, they don't need to tone down their feelings like they do with other people! A real love grows between two Virgos simply because they feel so at ease with one another. They will share many of their thoughts with one another and will spend a great deal of time in each other's company. However, they may both be just a little too edgy and highly strung to expose their hearts enough to ensure feelings of loving closeness. They have a rather disconcerting habit of picking at things that aren't quite right; they must both learn to relax and chill if their love is to blossom. What they need is some joint project, where they can put their organizational skills to work while doing something loving for one another, such as decorating their bedroom as the ultimate love palace. So long as they make the effort to get close to one another on an emotional level as well as on the mental and physical, this could become a very satisfying relationship.

 **In bed:** Lovemaking between a Virgo man and woman is no flash-in-the-pan quickie; these two will be at it for hours. This really builds the desire but it takes time to be so thorough, so they need to plan carefully for their encounters, and they no doubt will. They should stock up the refrigerator, put out the cat, and take the phone off the hook—and probably have the office phone numbers by the bed so that they can both call in sick the next day! That's the way lovemaking should be for these two; they're both into their physical, sensual pleasures, and sex is the one that intrigues them the most. They're both fascinated by the variety of different reactions that they can elicit from each other's bodies. Given a little time, they'll become so skilled in the art of sexual satisfaction that they could end up taking seconds rather than hours to complete their business—so efficiency has its drawbacks. This is definitely one tasty combination. However, since they both tend to be as open about their displeasure as they are about their pleasure, one or other of them could suffer from a loss of confidence. If they accept themselves and one other completely, then they'll have made the perfect match.

VIRGO WOMAN WITH **LIBRA MAN**

 **In love:** The Libra man is gifted with intelligence so he recognizes and admires the Virgo woman's mental agility. This makes for a strong initial attraction—they'll feel compelled to pick each other's brains for personal facts and general opinions. He's charming, clean, and

well-dressed, and is extremely pleased that she's always picture-perfect and takes such a pride in her appearance. One thing that's certain about this couple is that their life will run smoothly; bills will be paid on time, and their lovely home will never be untidy or allowed to fall down around their ears. They work well together to make a pleasing environment where they can settle down and enjoy each other's company. He'll accommodate her need to analyze his psyche and will find her modesty sweet and alluring. She'll be impressed by his refined, affable character and lofty ideas. This can be a perfect, mutually appreciative relationship—if only there were some spark. But that's not to say that it won't work. With so much that's right between them, it can't be wrong; simply ask Mr. Libra. He's already weighing up the pros and cons. No relationship is perfect but since these signs are next to one another in the zodiac, there's bound to be more than enough overlap to keep this couple running in a fuel-efficient mode for the rest of their lives. There's not much drama here, but who needs it when they can take the easy road together?

In bed: If the Virgo woman and Libra man were to start talking about how they would like to make love, it would certainly be a fun way to rev up their sexual motors. Both of them get very aroused by ideas, so the seduction could take place in their heads, which is titillating because of its ambiguity. Once the Virgo lady's engine is ready, she'll find out if he can live up to his promises, but if she's left idling for too long, her excitement could turn into an attack of self-doubt as to her

attractiveness. Things could stall at this point but he'll be ready to give it a jump-start if they do. Did he really need to head back to the kitchen, though, for the champagne and scented candles before climbing between the sheets? She should be flattered that he goes to so much trouble to make it a beautiful experience for her, so does she really need to start criticizing him? Unfortunately, to her interpretation, it wasn't her needs that he was being attentive to, but his own. And she was so looking forward to attending to him in her own special way. There's room here for both to fix things!

VIRGO WOMAN WITH **SCORPIO MAN**

In love: It really appeals to the Virgo woman's fantasy to be the maiden on whom the predatory Scorpio has set his sights, and this guy won't let her down on that score. He truly exudes a dangerous intensity when he's in seduction mode. Their courtship dance feels totally instinctive; whatever her age, she'll play the demure young woman who's unaware of the imminent threat to her innocence, yet she's just waiting for him. He'll play the dark prince who comes along and snatches her away from her virtuous existence. Although both are very self-contained during the initial stages of their courtship, that just raises their expectations for a truly deep involvement, but it can also make the Virgo lady a little nervous because there's a side of her that wants to remain detached from such an all-consuming passion. She knows it will be hard to keep her purity intact once the Scorpio man starts delving into her heart and soul, and yet

she is thrilled at the reaction she gets simply from being in his company. He instinctively senses her passionate side, which she keeps so well hidden; the idea of unlocking it will drive him crazy with desire! These two could easily get trapped together in a waltz, revolving around each other and getting deeper into each other's psyches to the exclusion of all else. It's a delicious feeling and should they ever part, they'll always be marked with the profound love that they once shared.

In bed: He's a really sexy beast! The Scorpio man seems to know just what to do to turn the Virgo woman into a quivering wench, wanton with desire. Her thoughts will naturally turn to eroticism wherever she is if there's a Scorpio lover by her side, and he'll be insatiable in his desire for her. These two seem to walk around in a world of their own, totally absorbed in each other's delectable sexiness. But they really should keep an eye out for those closed-circuit TV cameras! On the other hand, perhaps the cameras will add to the excitement! Another dimension to this partnership's sensual connection is that they both have inquiring minds, which means that they won't balk at exploring areas of their sexuality that others would be inclined to leave alone. They are, however, both sensitive enough to make sure that the other is completely comfortable with any experimentation. This very exclusive, private behavior between the two of them helps them to forge a truly deep and trusting bond.

VIRGO WOMAN WITH **SAGITTARIUS MAN**

In love: The love between a Virgo woman and a Sagittarius man is a strange one. In some ways they're totally compatible and get on really well together. He doesn't want an overly romantic partner, and is impressed by her capability, intelligence, and willingness to lend a hand when he's chasing down some new opportunity. She, meanwhile, is stimulated by his philosophical turn of mind and enjoys hearing all about his busy life without becoming jealous or resentful. She's a neatness freak, while he doesn't notice when things are messy or out of place, and although she likes things clean, and tidy, she doesn't appreciate having to pick up after him. She'll do it because it will drive her crazy to live in his mess, but she could end up resenting him for turning her into a criticizing nag. And if that's the way she behaves over half a dozen dirty coffee cups, then he'll soon fall out of love with her. She'll let him know what she expects but if she goes quiet on him, he could assume that her interest has turned elsewhere— though it might take him a while to notice! This partnership may never really get off the ground and live up to its potential, but there is such a thing as a Sagittarius man who will love and cherish his adorable Virgo lady enough to keep her happy. And she'll certainly be able to keep him happy!

In bed: The playful, adventurous Sagittarius man can be quite a turn-on for the demure, self-contained Lady Virgo. He's a bit of an Indiana Jones-type—a ruggedly masculine, philosophical adventurer,

who appeals both to her mind and her libidinous desires. But he's not in the habit of putting a lot of time into building up her passion. One or other of them will have to modify their expectations. If the Virgo lady can learn to initiate more than she normally would, then he'll rise to the occasion faster than a rocket. The Sagittarius man is so naturally lusty and spontaneous himself that he would love her to be ready at a moment's notice for a rumble in the jungle! When she is, it's great between them, but to really have her swinging like a primate, he needs to expend some energy on grooming her. He'll be happy to learn how, just for her benefit, but on those occasions when they just can't get their timing right, she'll be left standing on a precipice with only her ingenuity to get herself off.

VIRGO WOMAN WITH **CAPRICORN MAN**

In love: The ambitious, aspiring, expressive Goat couldn't do better than to have a Virgo woman by his side. He admires the way her clear-thinking brain works and the fact that she is capable and self-reliant, but what he really loves is her quiet allure and feminine charms. She'll enjoy helping her upwardly mobile Capricorn man to reach the goals he sets himself because he'll share every one of his achievements completely with her. She can see the detail that needs to be attended to along the way, while he focuses his attention on getting to the top. This is a mutually encouraging, wonderfully supportive partnership, and they find it really easy to love one another. Their connection goes beyond the creation of a

luxurious life filled with material things and status symbols, though they often both find that a very attractive by-product. These two are true soul mates; as soon as they meet, they feel spiritually at home. It's not something that they can put into words; it's just a feeling, a sense of a special compatibility between them. As well as being more interested in expanding their minds than their bank balances, they share a wickedly ironic sense of humor and an appreciation of the ridiculous. They find that, with each other more than with any other person, they can be playfully affectionate or seriously funny as the mood takes them. But best of all, when a loving, romantic mood washes over them, they can completely immerse themselves in one another.

 In bed: When Pan takes out his pipe, the Virgin dances to the tune, and the longer she dances, the more of a frenzy she'll find herself in. The Capricorn man has what it takes to get that white-hot fire burning inside the Virgo woman, and he's got the stamina to stoke the flames for hours. His intensely coiled sexuality and the steady rhythm of his sensuality will have her whirling like a dervish and will elicit unexpected responses, while no man could appreciate her skillful touch more than he does. This complete sense of physical connection is something he's longed to feel; it allows him to abandon his self-control, yet be himself and be totally self-indulgent. But this isn't about trying out new techniques or constantly assessing each other's performance; it's a real partnership whose growing intimacy is founded on a deep mutual respect that doesn't necessarily depend on sexual prowess. It's about an appreciation of the other's

gender—her gorgeous femininity, and his beautiful masculinity. That's what turns them on from the depths of their souls. When they make love, they see the innate beauty in one another as in the universe. This is as near divinity as it gets for two Earth signs. Yet they're both so realistic about their mutual attraction and desire for each other that they just know that they'll end up in bed together.

VIRGO WOMAN WITH **AQUARIUS MAN**

In love: The Virgo woman and Aquarius man will be totally intrigued by each other and could build up a fairly powerful connection based solely on a mutual need for stimulating conversation. The two of them will spend many a night curled up on the sofa, high on the excitement of tearing apart and putting back together conceptual ideas about the meaning of life and the universe. It makes her feel really special to have this knowledgeable man so intently focused on what she's saying; it means the world to her to be appreciated for her mind rather than her body. But though there's much that she admires in this man, and he in her, neither of them are well enough equipped to get into each other on every possible level. Both are truly independent, he perhaps more than she might expect, and this could lead to great expectations and little fulfillment. They both tend toward detachment, aloofness, and respect, so, although making a lasting emotional connection might take quite some time, if they both hang in there, they'll suddenly find that they've developed a

rather steady devotion to one another. But it's not easy for them to recognize whether they really feel something special for each other until it's perhaps too late. This is not one of those partnerships that just feels right from day one, but it's never really wrong either. It needs time and tenacity; eventually, the truth will out.

 **In bed:** It's a mutual mind thing between the Virgo woman and the Aquarius man. They're so attracted by each other's seemingly detached sexuality that it raises their expectations and libidos to high-voltage levels. When these two get into bed together, toys come in very useful. Not only do they help to satisfy their sexual needs, but they also provide hours of fun afterward when they take them apart to see how they work! This is sex, but not of the conventional sort. They both enjoy what it has to offer, and bed is the place where the Virgo woman will feel the deep connection to the Aquarius man that isn't all that evident during their conversations. He'll be totally turned on by her ability to light his fuse and she'll surprise him with her zealous hunger for his body. These two could reach stratospheric levels of erotic exploration when they're in bed together but it would require some lateral thinking on both their parts and a willingness to cater to each other's needs. She must have him totally, physically with her, and wanting and needing her; only then can she reveal to him just how deep her sexuality goes. She expects a lot from him but he'll quickly learn to live up to all her expectations!

VIRGO WOMAN WITH **PISCES MAN**

In love: The Virgo woman and her Pisces man are totally in sympathy with one another; in some ways they are like two peas in a pod. They have a peculiar sensitivity to each other, but while she's able to put it into words, he feels it intuitively. He has a unique talent for getting around her inhibitions without her even noticing; he simply seeps into her consciousness and soothes away all her nerves. He makes it so easy for her to express herself, and can help her to discover and enter her hidden depths and passions. She does as much for him by providing an anchor for his imaginative wanderings. No longer will his musings remain a dream; she can show him how to turn them into reality. Her ability to see things clearly helps to lift the fog from his eyes and she's so willing to offer practical assistance that he feels that, with her by his side, he could go anywhere and do anything. Before they know it, this couple will be in love. It won't matter what they do or where they go as long as they have each other. The years will fly by, they'll have many good times together, and soon they'll be a happy old couple enjoying the same feelings of mutual love and wonder that they experienced when they met fifty years before!

In bed: Since she's rather self-contained and a little nervous, it takes a very special lover to make the Virgo woman really relax and let go, but if she wants to take the plunge and jump right in with the Fish, then he'll take her on a magical journey of sensual joy and

sexual beauty. It genuinely pleases him to please her so he's totally willing to bring her to an ecstatic high. He'll want to nibble and taste every part of this woman, and she'll have no choice but to succumb to his gentle yet voracious desires. Being with the Pisces man will be a movingly emotional and spiritual experience, while he'll be so overwhelmed by her rapturous response to his touch that she'll almost have to fight for her turn to lavish her attentions on him. He needs to feel her physical presence and pleasure as much as she needs to feel his; it completes him and enraptures her. These two will learn a lot from each other about the art of lovemaking. He will school her in the delights of total surrender to the sensual experience and she'll show him a thing or two about how skillful touches, cleverly controlled, could rock his world and send him crashing into a new dimension of reality.

THE **VIRGO MAN** IN LOVE

It might take some time before the finer qualities of the Virgo man are appreciated. When he's in love he's very different from the fastidious man who can be spotted down at the local dry cleaner's picking up his work suit. He simply can't appear in all his glory until his heart has made a connection with a special lady or, indeed, with other people in general. He is a doting, devoted, and simply divine human being, and when he's in love, he's helpful to a fault. It's true that people talk about his difficult behavior and say that he's critical, exacting, and hard to please, but aren't these the same traits that anyone might adopt when they're feeling down? It can't be denied that the Virgo man is critical and exacting, but he works admirably hard, and carefully and precisely; the result is that he reaches a higher level of perfection than anyone else.

There is another way of looking at this: just as the Virgo man is an exacting perfectionist, so he's also capable of loving his lady in the most perfect and exacting manner! In love, he's as passionate and sensual as anyone, maybe even more so. He might like to have his sheets washed more often than most, but that's not so terrible when you think how much true love he has to offer. And alright, so he has to be in bed and asleep by a particular time because he's so health-conscious, but that doesn't mean that he can't continue the hanky-panky after he's had his morning muesli.

There is yet another way of looking at his gift for meticulousness: he can chart his way around a woman's body like a first-rate navigator and no, he

won't miss a single one of those special spots. It's in bed that his hidden treasures will be revealed, not only the treasures of his body, but those of his spirit, too. Once the Virgo man feels safe enough to open himself up and give himself completely, he'll reveal all his depth and passion; he'll quickly prove that he's a very keen lover who's capable of taking his special lady to heaven and back in one fell swoop! There are no pretences about him—he's 100 percent authentic. He's sensitive, too, which means that he's not a man to mess around with; he deserves to be cherished and adored for all his generosity of spirit.

However, make no mistake, this man is not an easy catch. It's true that he's very discriminating as to who he falls in love with, but he can't help it. It's not as if he stands there with a clipboard, checking off each woman he meets against his list of criteria. He's a man of the heart and it takes time before his heart is completely open, but once it is, there's no holding back. The Virgo man is dedicated, dependable, and sincere, and his love is deep, caring, and genuinely romantic. He's the real thing and worth keeping!

Virgo man with **ARIES WOMAN**

In love: The Virgo man with his modest and meticulous ways holds a strange fascination for the Aries woman. She's quieter, softer, and gentler in his company — at least for a while. She can appreciate that he's a clever man, able to dispel any uncertainties that arise in her life by analyzing, prioritizing, and organizing that life into a neat package. And because he appears to magically put things in order, she finds him fascinating, even compelling. He, on the other hand, sees her as a wonderfully unspoiled project, and is impressed by her directness, honesty, and innocence(!) He looks forward to unraveling her and putting her back together in a more refined, less erratic state. But nobody, not even the love of her life, is allowed to do that. She's nobody's pet project and she will resist, but that will just make her appeal to him even more. That is, of course, unless she has unleashed her famous Aries temper. Virgo men do not like to be criticized, particularly by a wildly angry, loud, and unladylike lover. They'll both sit down, talk it through, and come to a deeper understanding, but just a little of the shine will have rubbed off. It's a relationship that offers a learning experience for both, so if they're into lessons, they'll be in for the education of a lifetime. The contrast in their personalities will teach them all they need to know about themselves as individuals.

 **In bed:** He's born under the sign of the Virgin, but make no mistake, this isn't his first time, even though she would probably like it to be. Remember, the Aries woman wants the first bite of every cherry! Certainly, they can both pretend it's his first time every once in a while, and this will add to the excitement, besides, her flagrant freshness brings a sense of all that is new and untouched to every sexual encounter. The Virgo man is renowned for giving good service and works very well under direction. She, meanwhile, falls naturally into the role of leader and will be able to direct him so that he dutifully fulfills her desires. But don't get the idea that he doesn't move unless told to do so. He's no lap dog, although she wouldn't complain if he were! If he's left in charge, the Virgo man is capable of driving Ms. Aries into a flurry of delight. He'll get straight into her head for a start, and work his way down (via the heart, of course). He's subtle yet very sexual, explicit, and exacting—no part of the Aries woman will be left uncharted.

VIRGO MAN WITH **TAURUS WOMAN**

 **In love:** Since both the Taurus woman and the Virgo man are rather cautious, it would be unusual to find these two in bed together by the end of their first date. They are much more likely to spend their time finding out if they have any interests in common. Once they get beyond their initial reticence—particularly the reticence of the Virgo man—there will be some very sultry signals sent out. It won't take

too long for them to grow really fond of one another and build a very solid foundation of love. Born under the sign of the Virgin, the Virgo man's innocence appeals to the Taurus woman, but make no mistake, he's not that innocent. Virgo man is really much more knowing about what makes people tick and what captures their hearts than he lets on. Both of these players have a peaceful disposition, which is always an inducement to love. The Virgo man offers intelligent conversation, while the Taurus woman gives him the tranquillity and understanding he needs. She may get a little sore at his finicky, fastidious ways, and by the fact that he occasionally criticizes everything from her choice of home decoration to her deodorant. In turn, he may take exception to her self-indulgent lazing around in front of the television when it's her turn to do the dishes. But with both of them being Earth signs, they have a natural affinity. They'll not only like one other: given the chance, they'll adore one another, too.

In bed: The passionate Virgo man has hidden depths, but he'll be far more interested in finding hers. This will certainly raise his interest and, being the helpful sort, he'll always be willing to give a hand! Virgos are known for their skillful manual dexterity and the Taurus woman need not be shy about making use of his craftsmanship. She'll also find that he's very good at following instructions. She's so sexy that just her touch makes his heart beat faster, but her powerful sensuality will calm his nerves, massage away any tension, and help to ease him into a gentle rhythm. Seriously, these two are real earth-movers, and since that always requires a

slow start, foreplay is definitely on their sexual menu. Speaking of menus, only the tastiest and most delectable morsels will do. And since she does require her man to have stamina, she will happily provide him with plenty of delicious treats, fed lovingly from her own hand, to help him keep his strength up. Once the Taurus woman and Virgo man are both intoxicated with the foods of love—consumed slowly, with every mouthful savored— they'll be ready to indulge each other in the extreme. Both can relish this moving experience.

ViRGO mAn WiTH GEmiNi WOmAN

 **In love:** Both Gemini and Virgo are ruled by Mercury, the planet of communication, information, and adaptability, so there will be certain signals passed between the Gemini woman and the Virgo man that others just can't pick up on. Whether these signals have anything to do with love, however, is another thing, though there is a connection, which at least promotes conversation. After a while they could get used to each other's ways of communicating and chances become higher that they'll fall in love. Having been born under an Earth sign, the Virgo man is sensual and sensitive to what moves the Gemini lady. He cherishes her by giving her all his tender loving, but it may be a touch too much. She might not know how to handle herself in the face of so much genuine sentimentality. Sure, he has a sense of humor, but he's serious when it comes to love, while she prefers to make light of the whole thing, even though she is capable of

making the Virgo man feel warmly loved. This is a mentally stimulating combination but the Gemini woman will need to practice speaking from the heart rather than the head, and the somewhat practical Virgo man needs to try not to pin her down to one point of view. Celebrating the other's differences while feeling cozy about the mercurial similarities that exist between them is a great start. Once they get the hang of it, the love they make will carry more intensity, warmth, and meaning.

In bed: Both the Virgo man and Gemini woman will have read all the instruction manuals, from *The Kama Sutra* to the latest kinky stuff. They'll know which bit goes nicely where, and what just causes friction, and as their love grows, the motions will become less mechanical. Mercury is the planetary ruler of both Gemini and Virgo but, unlike all the other planets, Mercury doesn't have a gender, so role reversal is common when the Gemini woman and Virgo man get between the sheets. It doesn't matter who is on top, who comes or goes first, or who is inside or out. When they get tired of one position they can always switch to another. However, Gemini is likely to get bored more quickly than Virgo, and will want to move at dizzying speed through a series of complex poses designed to keep her man excited. But sometimes, the opposite effect is the result, because at the heart of a Virgo man's sexuality is a desire to get to the bottom of things and really understand the workings of each physical sensation. One way of keeping her still while he employs his skills is to whisper a stream of fantastical, titillating possibilities and proposals in her ear.

This sort of mental gymnastics will always act as a distraction. And the way for the Gemini lady to keep her Virgo man's attention is to try to indulge him with a little more e-motion, not just the latest motions. He's generous in bed and deserves a lot in return.

VIRGO MAN WITH **CANCER WOMAN**

 **In love:** There's an easy, peaceful feeling about the love between a Cancer woman and a Virgo man. They're unlikely to ever let each other down. In fact, they very quickly get into a harmonious rhythm that flows sweetly through the relationship so, "if music be the food of love, play on." Theirs will be a playful relationship—they share a sense of friendly amusement about the oddities of life and enjoy one another's endearing idiosyncrasies. They are indulgent of each other's foibles and often find that some gentle teasing makes for a lighthearted bonding experience. Both are liable to get crabby at times, but if ever there was someone who could make them laugh, then that someone is the other. This is a beautifully symbiotic relationship in which each fits the other's vibe perfectly. Although she can be grumpy and he can be critical, when they're together, their need to sulk or pick will melt away. They're good for each other and their love keeps their hearts happy and healthy. The laughter and companionship they share have a powerful healing effect and the mutual support they gain from the relationship gives them the courage to go beyond their normal bounds of personal achievement and to revolutionize and revitalize their lives.

In bed: She could get moody, which could cause him to chill or make him start picking on her for being so changeable. He could get critical, which would cause her to retreat into her shell and stay there until he apologizes. But they know each other well, so this behavior could actually be part of their routine, and because there is so much love between them, neither can take any of it too seriously. Funnily enough, these very frustrations are the appetizer to their feast. Despite appearances, a little bit of tension is just what the Cancer woman and Virgo man need to increase their desire to get into each other's arms. They actually enjoy a minor disagreement because of the making-up bit that always comes along afterward. The result of all this is a desperate hunger for each other. The sex is satisfying and comforting—a staple part of their relationship. The Cancer woman has enough flowing sensuality to reach into the depths of her Virgo man's passion, and he'll go weak at the knees and blissfully fall apart as she gently coaxes him to become one with her. The more he holds her and enjoys her sweet caresses, the more he is able to feed her desire and heighten his own. With such mutually responsive passion, it's hard for them to tell where one begins and the other finishes.

VIRGO MAN WITH LEO WOMAN

In love: At first glance, the Leo woman together with the Virgo man epitomize success in love. Theirs is a passionate, yet practical set-up. He'll be very supportive of her, encouraging her in her

career and helping out at home, for who could fail to want to help a Leo woman? After all, she's royalty! He'll be enamored with her warm smile, her big personality, her presence, and her sense of command, and he'll dote on her completely. She'll offer him the loyalty and prestige that he desires and deserves. These two could really depend on one another and could make a habit of it. But there's a catch: when Virgo man wants to assert his masculine nature, he might feel that she doesn't need him as much as he would like. She might make him feel like the mouse that her fantastic feline self has trapped only in order to feed her needs. But he's smart enough to stay ahead of the game and could lead her on a merry chase now and then. Her tenacity in holding onto him should be all he needs to confirm she loves him but, being extremely bright and a stickler for detail, he may attempt to hold his own by dropping hints about the areas in which she isn't quite coming up to scratch. That's a very dangerous game to play unless he wants to have his eyes scratched out—Lady Lions don't take criticism well.

In bed: The Virgo man is far less spontaneous than the Leo woman and much, much subtler, but make no mistake, this man is no mouse. He's capable of making her wilder than she already is, and that's no small feat. His tickling, teasing style is very different from hers and it really turns her on, while her passionate, voracious style will very quickly arouse his interest. Since the Lady Leo loves to be adoringly admired, she may well put on a show to turn him on and he'll be an avid watcher, before quickly joining in. The Virgo man needs her fire to melt his resistance

and allow his sensuality to surface, but that takes time, so she'll have to be careful not to burn herself out in the process. However, once he discovers that deep reservoir of passion within himself, he'll devote all of it to her service, falling on his knees and worshiping her regal presence.

VIRGO MAN WITH **VIRGO WOMAN**

See pages 63–64.

VIRGO MAN WITH **LIBRA WOMAN**

In love: The Libra lady won't even realize when the Virgo man draws her in. He's so subtle and she's so susceptible to his charm. He appeals to her mind; in fact, he will show her from the start that he loves her way of thinking. She can wax lyrical with him and he'll listen, encouraging her and paying her the compliments that she really needs to hear. She just knows that there's more to him than meets the eye. There's a genuinely loving compatibility between these two: they'll never have to remind each other to pick up their dirty socks from the floor, for example! He finds her charm and grace irresistible and can hardly wait to get her on her own, but sometimes they'll get so bound up in discussing ideals and the way things should be, that they never actually get around to making things happen between them. The Libra lady is idealistic and aims high, while he wants to win the world for her—unfortunately this isn't really within the

realms of possibility, so there could be some disappointment. So long as they both want the same things out of life, they'll find in each other a supporting partner, but the moment their goals differ, then things may go pear-shaped. Although she'll appear to take his criticisms with good grace and will make the necessary adjustments, if there's one thing out of balance about a Libra lady, then she'll shift the burden of blame right back in his direction and he'll find he's made a rod for his own back.

 **In bed:** The Virgo man loves sex—pure, perfect sex. The Libra lady is one purring sex kitten—she definitely won't be able to stop herself from rubbing up against him. This is the man who'll simply adore seeing the loving Libra lady dressed in virginal lacy white lingerie and she will no doubt be happy to oblige. It will appeal both to her fantasy notions of romance and to his libido if she lies invitingly on the bed, looking like a work of art while he studies every inch of her with his artisan eyes and touches her with his deft craftsman fingers. He's earthy, real, and thorough as well as sensually switched on, so he'll do anything she needs. He'll quickly find that his ability to focus his efforts fully on the little things brings very satisfactory results. She'll never leave him high and dry, and though what he offers her may not be spiritual or even emotional, it will certainly be stimulating in all the right places. He gets to her on the physical level and she gets to him on the mental level. He likes the fact that she's rather vocal and enjoys telling him her fantasies almost as much as she likes the clever way he makes his actions fit her words.

VIRGO MAN WITH SCORPIO WOMAN

In love: The Scorpio woman is instinctive and she'll have recognized from the very beginning that there's much more to the Virgo man than is apparent on the surface. She likes depth, and he has it. Being with him is like having a therapy session; all sorts of buried urges start revealing themselves. He can't help himself when faced with her intense, penetrating mind; she frightens and fascinates him in equal measure. It's very thrilling. She'll love the way he responds to her on all levels and knows that she can get under his aloof exterior better than anyone. There's a very obvious sense of compatibility between these two, no matter what circumstances they find themselves in. In fact, they could become rather obsessive about each other to the exclusion of all else. When it comes to the long term, he's very good at organizing the practical, day-to-day necessities, which leaves her free to take care of the little things that add spice to the relationship—the Scorpio lady has a bottomless reserve of spicy ideas. The only downside is that, though he's pretty adaptable, he'll resent any efforts by her to control or manipulate him. If she tries, that could make him want to create some distance between them, which he'll do by revealing that slightly over-critical side of his nature. And if she perceives that he might be censuring her, then the Virgo man will soon feel that penetrating sting in the Scorpion tail, and boy, will it hurt!

In bed: The Scorpio woman is just the one to unlock the Virgo man's deeply sexual tendencies. Is he Virgo the Virgin? Definitely not. He's hot—white hot, but he needs a woman like a Scorpio to set him alight. She won't believe what this man is capable of arousing in her when they get locked in the bedroom. She'll feel pure, unadulterated passion that keeps on burning until she can't stand it any more; she just won't know what's gotten into her! The Scorpio woman simply wells up with erotic energy at his slightest touch, while the Virgo man has skills that could surprise even the Scorpio lady. This is one time when he doesn't mind getting dirty, especially when it comes to talking, but he's also open to other suggestions simply because he finds her such a turn-on. She could persuade him to try anything, at least once. When it comes to the physical expression of their feelings, these two are in perfect accord. He'll be truly awash with loving feelings induced by her powerful yet embracing emotions, just as she will be touched by the way he conveys his gentle but strong need for her.

VIRGO MAN WITH **SAGITTARIUS WOMAN**

In love: This is a complicated coupling but it's not impossible. The Virgo man loves the Sagittarius lady's adventurous soul, but persuading him to go along with her would be like trying to teach him to be footloose and fancy-free—it's simply not something he does. However much spontaneity appeals to him in theory, in practice he feels the pull to remain grounded. Trying to tame the Sagittarius woman would be like

trying to domesticate a tiger; there's a wild side to her that must remain free to range wherever her soul leads. He admires her optimism, but at times he attacks it with his cynical humor. His cleverness and ability to organize all the practical issues of daily life will attract the Archer lady; that's what she needs, in fact, so he's very good for her. Her attention is so often focused on the big picture that she trips herself up on the little details that he is so skillful at tidying away. Love may grow, but she'll have to tend it well if she wants it to flower, since his nerves may not be able to take too much of her wild unpredictability. Unfortunately, there's a chance that they'll both be so caught up in doing their own thing that they'll forget to merge their interests, and once they let the relationship slide, they'll have a difficult time getting it back. On the plus side, at a mental level this is a great partnership. She's the one with the wicked sense of humor and he's the one with the dry wit. They love to laugh together and will do so often.

In bed: The Sagittarius lady will love the ardor and bliss that the Virgo man offers between the sheets. This man might be from the element of Earth but he can certainly match her fire with his physical passion. It's definitely in him to get very involved in the sexual process but if she wants to release that bubbling erotic energy that he keeps so well hidden, it will take some persistent effort. She doesn't usually see the point in being subtle when it comes to expressing her lusty desires, but if she's hunting a Virgo then the game is more one of hide-and-seek than kiss-chase. He needs to remember to focus on the whole woman, not just on

the sweet bits that he finds so delectable. Time will probably show that though this relationship is good in many ways, in the end, it may lack the right kind of friction. They'll certainly be able to enjoy games in bed but it's the daytime antics that threaten to spoil the anticipation of the night's excitement. Their individual methods of seduction just don't seem to spark the ignition without a little tinkering to get their motors running. But if the Sagittarius lady likes to travel and can go the extra mile with her Virgo man, then he'll definitely take the brakes off.

ViRGO mAn WiTH **CAPRiCORn WOMAn**

 In love: There's a natural sense of intimacy between a Virgo man and Lady Capricorn. When they go to a party together, though they might split and do their own mingling, they feel the confidence and security of knowing that they'll be back together at the end. In fact, they're so in tune with each other that if one of them needs saving from the bore in the corner, the other will know instinctively and rescue will be just around the corner. With their sense of trust and mutual affection they feel good being together anywhere. The success rate for the Virgo man with the Capricorn woman is very high; the only possible problem might be that they're both so conscientious toward everyone else that they might find it difficult making the time for their own special, intimate moments. Theirs is a very natural love; it just feels so right and is creative in the sense that this is a partnership that has the potential to be much bigger than the sum of its

parts. Although it may take the Virgo man a little longer to really commit than the Capricorn woman would like, she's patient and already knows in her bones what he'll realize soon enough—that she has what he wants and needs and that he loves her for having it.

In bed: The sensuality between the Virgo man and Capricorn woman is tangible—it sits like a solid wall of sexual energy simply waiting to be scaled so the heights of erotic pleasure can be attained. Their lovemaking is so intense that it will leave both of them breathless and panting from their exertions. This is very satisfying sex; it's lovemaking for real. They don't need any gadgets, toys, or fantasies but nor will they reject them out of hand because these two feel more playful when wrapped in each other's arms than at any other time. This is what bonds them for life. As a lover, he'll be so attentive to her requirements that she'll respond like never before, which is what he needs to get in touch with the essence of his own sexuality. Virgo man can take a long time to really explode with passion, so her patience and prowess will pay off. She's the girl who can release him from his need for self-control, and he's the man who'll entice her to reach greater heights than she ever thought possible. And when that happens the earth will shake. It will definitely be worth the effort, though it won't seem like an effort—more like a pleasure. The best part is that these two will never tire of one another.

VIRGO MAN WITH **AQUARIUS WOMAN**

 In love: This is a meeting of minds, with both openly admiring the other for their amicability, intelligence, and communication skills. It's likely to be the combination of the inventive ideas of the Aquarius woman and the detailed elaborations of the Virgo man that brings them together and has them spending night after night indulging in exciting philosophical and psychological conversations. The constant reshaping of their thoughts will keep them together for some time but theirs is unlikely to be a great romance or a grand passion. It's more likely to be a solid friendship, since intelligent conversation is important to both. They'll get plenty out of it when they're together, but it won't be easy for either to commit to this relationship because both remain a little aloof from expressing their emotions. Love can grow between them even though it may never really be earth-shattering. They may feel that there must be something more, which is sad as they've come so far; the compatibility is there and that's not an easy thing to find. She might not like it when he gets picky because that draws her down avenues of thought where she doesn't want to go, and the same will be true for him when she comes up with some of her more eccentric ideas. They'll be friends forever; both are so easygoing that they just can't help but like each other enormously, but love? Well, that may be a tall order unless there's some deeper connection.

In bed: The foreplay of these two will be truly fantastic. With their sexy verbal banter both have a way of winding the other up into a state of expectation and excitement. They'll find it teasing and tantalizing to imagine the sexual talents that the other possesses and they can really get each other into a frenzy of jittery anticipation, but somehow, the idea of sex together is so much better than the reality. If the Aquarius woman spends too long with the Virgo man as her lover, she might begin to climb the walls in frustration. She's naturally very loyal but variety is the spice of her life and although he's rather versatile, his efficiency will eventually become too predictable for her. Meanwhile, the Virgo man can pick up a complex quicker than he can catch a cold and unless she knows how to build up his ego, he might just whimper and run away, which is not what she wants. He deserves more and so does she. It can work between them but they both need to make a conscious effort to tune in to each other and to stay that way. They're both so cool that they need to work at raising the sensual heat above tepid.

VIRGO MAN WITH PISCES WOMAN

In love: The Pisces woman just knows that there's more to this guy than meets the eye, and there's certainly more than he's willing to reveal. But she's the girl who can ease her way around his detachment and help to unlock his emotions—and boy, does he need help! So does she when it comes to all those practical, mundane matters that

he's so good at; this gentle guy can help to ground her in reality and stop her drifting about. This makes for a very nice arrangement. What he lacks, she has more than enough of and what she lacks, he has in sackfuls. As opposite signs of the zodiac they complement each other perfectly, but he may not be very willing to share all he has with the Lady Fish at first—he's very good at compartmentalizing the separate areas of his life, while she needs to flow through it all unhindered. At worst, this could lead to a deadly silence between them; if she feels that he's keeping things from her then she may not be willing to share her secrets with him and so he'll miss out on all the wondrous experiences that these two could have together. So long as she doesn't take his initial reticence and criticisms too much to heart, and so long as he doesn't try to meddle in those areas of her life where she prefers to float free, then their love could grow not only into a thing of beauty, but into something that heals all ills and soothes all pain.

In bed: The earthy Virgo man can take a little while to get going in the bedroom because he's often shy, but the Pisces woman understands shyness. Once she goes to work on him he'll get going very quickly—and keep right on going. He can be insatiable with the right lover, and it just so happens that she's the one. They fit together like a hand in a glove. Together, they are pure, pulsating passion, which is a pleasant surprise for them both. These two may not hit it off on the first try, but because they have a sort of compulsion to be together, they'll probably try again and again, and each time it will simply get more explosive. There will

be moments when the Pisces woman feels as though she's naked in a field of wild flowers on a hot summer afternoon—excited yet enraptured and enjoying a delightfully naughty sense of freedom. Being with her when she's like this will make the Virgo man wild with desire. Fantasy turns into reality when a Pisces woman turns to her Virgo man for sex. This relationship is very erotic, amazingly spiritual, sweetly emotional, and unbelievably satisfying.

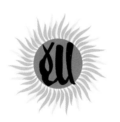